THE EASY CREOLE AND CAJUN COOKBOOK

The Easy Creole and Cajun Cookbook

MODERN AND CLASSIC DISHES MADE SIMPLE

Ryan Boudreaux

Photography by
Andrew Purcell

ROCKRIDGE
PRESS

For general information on our other products and services or to obtain technical support, please contact our Customer Care Department within the United States at (866) 744-2665, or outside the United States at (510) 253-0500.

Rockridge Press publishes its books in a variety of electronic and print formats. Some content that appears in print may not be available in electronic books, and vice versa.

TRADEMARKS: Rockridge Press and the Rockridge Press logo are trademarks or registered trademarks of Callisto Media Inc. and/or its affiliates, in the United States and other countries, and may not be used without written permission. All other trademarks are the property of their respective owners. Rockridge Press is not associated with any product or vendor mentioned in this book.

Interior and Cover Designer: Sean Doyle
Art Producer: Hannah Dickerson
Editor: Britt Bogan
Production Manager: Giraud Lorber
Production Editor: Melissa Edeburn
Photography © 2020 Andrew Purcell. Food styling by Carrie Purcell. Author photo courtesy of Monique Boudreaux.
Cover Recipe: Shrimp, Sausage, and Grits, page 51

ISBN: Print 978-1-64739-337-3 | Ebook 978-1-64739-338-0
R0

I dedicate this cookbook to my dear heart, bride, best friend, and sous chef, **Monique Boudreaux**. Her love, support, assistance, encouragement, cooking, and tasting is forever cherished.

CONTENTS

INTRODUCTION

I have always been fascinated with food and cooking, and my passion continues to be an integral part of my Boudreaux family heritage. I've taught myself many cuisines, and I still love to try out new gastronomies. About 12 years ago, I created my blog, Cajun Chef Ryan (CajunChefRyan.com), with the tagline, "Feeling and sharing a world of cooking—more than your average Cajun." I started the blog as a way to preserve and share my 37 years of experience and collected recipes from my home, my family, and the restaurant industry, which I serve as a professional chef. Many recipes that my grandmothers and great-grandmothers made are still awaiting their rightful place in the digital world.

I have fond memories of Sadie "Momom" Boudreaux's potato salad, divinity candy, pecan pies, and gumbo. I remember Uncle Buford Boudreaux preparing smoked and barbecue venison, chicken, and sausages, and his wonderful country gumbo. My dad made the best slow charcoal-roasted barbecue half chicken I have ever eaten. My mother's drunken shrimp and garlic-roasted pork loin were always dinner favorites. Her fabulous dilly bread, with dill weed and cottage cheese, ignited my passion for understanding yeast and how it works.

This book contains many 30-minute and one-pot recipes created with the home cook in mind. Some are one-pot *and* 30-minute recipes, which means less mess, less prep, and less time until dinner is on the table. All include ingredients you can find at any grocery store, but if you're interested in incorporating ingredients that may be less familiar to you, see the recipe tips for substitutions.

I hope you enjoy preparing these dishes my family and I have loved for decades and continue to serve at gatherings. I'm celebrating and sharing with you many years of happy cooking and bon appétit.

CHAPTER 1

WELCOME TO CAJUN AND CREOLE COOKING

Louisiana Cajun and Creole culture originates in the bayous and waterways of South Louisiana and the Mississippi Delta. Although deeply rooted in traditions handed down from generation to generation, Cajun and Creole cooking has evolved and today reflects Italian, German, Vietnamese, French, African, Caribbean, and South American influences.

Today the world of Cajun and Creole cooking is far-reaching. You can sample it as far away as Somers Point, New Jersey, which holds a Cajun Festival every February; Longview, Texas, where a parade rolls along with Cajun cuisine the Saturday before Mardi Gras; or at a restaurant in Puyallup, Washington, that churns out classic New Orleans dishes and cocktails. From coast to coast, Americans enjoy the spicy, tasty, delectable, sweet, and sometimes decadent, self-indulgent flavors that make up Cajun and Creole cooking.

THE BASICS OF CAJUN AND CREOLE COOKING

Cajun cooking developed from the descendants of French colonists who settled in Acadia in the Canadian provinces in the 17th century. In the mid-1770s the colonists were expelled during French–English hostilities, and they migrated to South Louisiana. Some Cajuns, especially those born in the New World, called themselves *Creole*. This French term, borrowed from Spanish and Portuguese, means "born in the new world." Others who self-identify with Creole include Spanish and Latin American cultures who settled in South Louisiana during the same time.

Cajun and Creole cooking is more than the sum of the food, ingredients, and preparation methods that make up a recipe. It also includes Louisiana culture, natural resources of the South, and the seasons that produce a variety of fresh fruits, vegetables, meats, and seafood in the region. Walk into most home gardens and you'll find okra, tomatoes, and eggplant; varieties of squash from acorn to zucchini; collards, mustards, turnip greens, and Swiss chard; the Cajun Trinity of onions, celery, and bell peppers; and peppers ranging from hot to mild to sweet, such as jalapeño, cayenne, habanero, ancho, poblano, and banana. Meats from a Cajun butcher shop include a wide range of pork cuts, like bacon, fat back, ribs, pork loin, pork chops, pork shoulder, andouille sausage, Tasso ham, smoked sausage links, breakfast sausage patties, crackling pork, smoked ribs, and pulled pork. And let's not forget about the abundance of seafood found along the coastal waterways, byways and the Gulf of Mexico, starting with those favorite bivalves, the Gulf oyster. These sweet and salty, plump and juicy, ready-for-dipping-in-cocktail-sauce delicacies are not to be missed. Shrimp, another bounty of the sea, range from brown to white depending on the source and season and come in many sizes.

KITCHEN EQUIPMENT FOR CAJUN AND CREOLE COOKING

A well-stocked kitchen is critical for the home cook, as you need the right tools to turn out successful dishes. Cajun and Creole cooking is no exception. I've listed the essential equipment, plus a list of optional pieces that are not always necessary but make good additions to your wish list.

Essentials

These tools are the most essential pieces of kitchen equipment you'll need to get started on the path of Cajun and Creole cooking.

- **Large cast-iron skillet.** A well-seasoned large cast-iron skillet is essential for blackening fish, chicken, and steak. You can use this multipurpose pan on stovetops, grills, and wood-burning fires as well as in the oven.

- **Dutch oven (3-quart).** A 3-quart Dutch oven with a tight-fitting lid is a must for soups and stews. Like the cast-iron skillet, you can use this on the stovetop, on a grill, and in the oven.

- **Stockpot (8-quart).** A large, heavy, lined stockpot that can hold at least 8 quarts (2 gallons) is best for making chicken, beef, seafood, and vegetable stocks. To get 1 gallon of stock, you need enough volume to hold all the ingredients and room for the liquid to simmer for several hours without evaporating. This pot is also great for making soups and stews.

- **Chef knife.** If you have only one knife, make sure it's a high-quality sharp chef knife. I'd say I do 99 percent of my knife work in the kitchen with my 10-inch chef knife. Good-quality brands include Henckels, Victorinox, and Wüsthof. You'll do most of your chopping, dicing, and slicing with your chef knife, and it can't be beat for flexibility and all-around usefulness. Heck, I've even seen a chef use one to trim down a whole beef tenderloin.

- **Roasting pan (9-by-13-inch).** Make sure you have at least one 9-by-13-inch roasting pan with sides that are at least 3 inches high.

Optional

Optional kitchen items that are good to have but not essential include:

- **Baking sheets.** You'll find that 18-by-24-inch baking sheets are great for baking, roasting, and setting up cold or prepped items.

- **Meat thermometer.** A probe meat thermometer is a foolproof way to determine whether your meat is done. It also prevents overcooking and ensures you're heating foods to the proper internal temperature.

- **Food processor.** For a smooth cream soup or hummus, the food processor is a handy tool that makes quick prep of most recipes.

Pumpkin Seed and Cheddar Cornbread Muffins 65

KITCHEN STAPLES

A well-stocked pantry is the start to great food and easy preparation. Here is a list of the produce, meat and seafood, pantry goods, and spices and other items used in the recipes in this book.

Produce

- **Cajun Trinity (onions, celery, bell peppers):** Used in many Cajun and Creole dishes

- **Garlic:** Make sure you have plenty; you'll use double or triple the amount called for in typical recipes.

- **Okra:** A favorite in gumbo but used in other recipes

- **Parsley:** Not only a garnish, but also adds delicate flavor

- **Scallions:** Adds great flavor and makes a wonderful garnish

Meat and Seafood

- **Andouille or smoked sausage:** These sausages are interchangeable and used in many dishes.

- **Bacon:** Rendered bacon fat adds so much flavor to any sautéed dish.

- **Crabmeat:** These delicate, luscious morsels are always a delight in soups and stuffings.

- **Crawfish or shrimp:** Otherwise known as the bounty of the sea, crawfish and shrimp are interchangeable in the recipes that follow.

- **Oysters:** Raw, baked, or chargrilled, this bivalve is a must in your cooking arsenal.

- **Spiced or Tasso ham:** Turn up the heat in your recipe with some of this highly spiced pork.

Pantry Goods

- **Converted rice, jasmine rice, basmati rice:** Cajuns and Creoles love their rice—put any sauce on top and it's good eating.

- **Diced tomatoes:** Many of these recipes use diced tomatoes, so keep a few cans on hand.

- **Prepared horseradish:** You'll need this ingredient for cocktail sauce.

- **Tomato-based chili sauce:** The classic cocktail sauce would not exist without this ingredient.

- **Worcestershire sauce:** This sauce is my secret ingredient in many recipes.

Spices and Other Items

- **Basil:** This classic herb is included in many recipes.

- **Cayenne pepper:** Need I say more? Cajun 101 here.

- **Filé powder:** This rich, flavorful herbal powder is an essential gumbo spice usually added at the end of cooking.

- **Hot sauce:** You can add this sauce to dishes such as jambalaya, gumbo, or étouffée, or just dash a few drops in your gumbo or over your red beans and rice. I like Crystal Hot Sauce, which is made in New Orleans.

- **Oregano:** This spice is used in many Cajun and Creole dishes.

- **Pickled peppers in vinegar:** Sprinkle some spicy vinegar over your red beans and enjoy.

- **Smoked paprika:** This spice adds great smoke flavor.

- **Thyme:** This spice is perfect for étouffée, gumbo, and jambalaya.

CHAPTER 2

FOUNDATIONS OF CAJUN AND CREOLE FARE

Classic Cajun and Creole recipes usually start with essentials like roux, stocks, spice blends, and the Cajun Trinity. A roux thickens and adds flavor. This chapter includes recipes for three types of roux: quick, blond, and dark. For soups, sauces, and stews, stocks provide additional flavor you just can't get from water. You'll find great recipes for chicken, beef, vegetable, and seafood stocks. Spice blends are another foundation for Cajun and Creole cooking, and Cajun Spice Blend, Grill Barbecue Rub, and Creole Spice Blend are used repeatedly in these recipes. Store the spice blends for several months at room temperature in a cool pantry out of direct sunlight.

Vegetable Stock, page 17

ROUX

A roux thickens a dish and enhances its flavor. It's typically found in recipes for soups, sauces, stews, gumbo, étouffée, and stuffings. A roux is always a one-to-one ratio (weight or volume) of flour to fat. You can use any fat to make a roux, including peanut oil, bacon fat, duck fat, chicken fat, butter, and margarine. If you want to create a deeper flavor profile in your dish, use a roux made from animal fat.

Three elements of a roux change as it continues to cook are: the color darkens, the flavor becomes richer and nuttier, and the thickening property diminishes because the gluten and protein in the flour break down.

QUICK ROUX

When you're short on time and need a quick roux, this one gets your recipe started in a jiffy. This basic roux is perfect for thickening soup, béchamel (milk-based) sauce, or any other sauce you need to make in a hurry. It does not cook very long so you won't achieve a deep flavor, but you will get the full thickening power of the flour. **MAKES 1 CUP**

PREP TIME: 5 minutes | **COOK TIME:** 10 minutes

½ **cup peanut oil, bacon fat, or butter**

½ **cup flour**

1. In a large nonstick pan, heat the oil or fat, or melt the butter.

2. Stir in the flour until it is incorporated and the mixture is smooth. Continue to cook over medium-low heat, stirring continuously, for 6 to 8 minutes, until the roux has thickened and the flour has cooked.

STORAGE TIP: Use the roux immediately in any recipe that calls for a quick roux. Store in a sealed mason jar in the refrigerator for up to 1 month or in the freezer for up to 3 months.

PREPARATION TIP: For an even faster roux, whisk together the fat and flour in a microwave-safe bowl, then microwave for 1 minute, remove, and stir. Return to the microwave for 1 more minute, then remove and stir again. Repeat once more. Let cool before using.

BLOND ROUX

Blond roux is one of the most widely used of the roux family. It thickens cream-based soups, such as Oyster Artichoke Soup (page 49), and milk- or dairy-based sauces, like béchamel sauce. Blond roux is not as dark as other roux, but it does start to take on a hint of color (hence the name). Blond roux has a nuttier flavor than a quick roux and retains almost as much thickening power. **MAKES 1 CUP**

PREP TIME: 5 minutes | **COOK TIME:** 25 minutes

½ cup peanut oil, bacon fat, or butter

½ cup flour

1. In a large nonstick pan, heat the oil or fat, or melt the butter.

2. Stir in the flour until it is incorporated and the mixture is smooth. Continue to cook over medium-low heat, stirring continuously, for 20 minutes, or until the roux has thickened, the flour has cooked, and the color is light but not burned.

STORAGE TIP: Use the roux immediately in any recipe that calls for a quick roux. Store in a sealed mason jar in the refrigerator for up to 1 month or in the freezer for up to 3 months.

PREPARATION TIP: Be sure to give the roux your undivided attention. Stirring constantly ensures an evenly cooked roux without burned specks of flour.

DARK ROUX

ONE POT

Found in recipes for gumbo, sauce piquant, étouffée, and other Cajun and Creole preparations, the dark roux is full of nutty, toasty flavor that adds richness to any dish. As the roux continues to cook you will notice that its aroma starts to take on a nutty bouquet like toasted almonds. This is a sign it's almost done. **MAKES 1 CUP**

PREP TIME: 5 minutes | **COOK TIME:** 45 minutes

½ cup peanut oil, bacon
   fat, or butter
½ cup flour

1. In a large nonstick pan, heat the oil or fat, or melt the butter.

2. Stir in the flour until it is incorporated and the mixture is smooth. Continue to cook over medium-low heat, stirring continuously, for 30 to 45 minutes, or until the flour has cooked and the color is dark but not burned.

3. Remove from the heat. To avoid any splatter, let cool before adding to any preparation.

STORAGE TIP: Store in a sealed mason jar in the refrigerator for up to 1 month or in the freezer for up to 3 months.

PREPARATION TIP: Start with a wire whisk to incorporate the flour and fat. Once all the lumps are out of the flour, switch to a wooden spoon or, better yet, a wooden paddle. The paddle makes it easier to ensure you are stirring the bottom of the pan and helps prevent burning.

STOCK

A good stock is an essential ingredient for laying the foundation of your Cajun and Creole cooking. It adds so much flavor to sauces, soups, stews, gumbos, and other dishes. In addition to the main flavoring from the bones, most stocks include onions, celery, carrots, parsley, garlic, fresh herbs, and other seasonings. For vegetable stock, you can add a host of other vegetables, including greens, vegetable tops (like carrot, beet, and radish), broccoli bottoms, cauliflower cores, cabbage, and anything else you have on hand.

Stocks can seem like mysterious concoctions and they instill fear in many, but they are actually simple one-pot recipes. When cooking stock, it generally takes as long as 12 hours and as little as 1 hour to complete the flavor-extraction process. Beef stock requires the most time, and seafood stock cooks most quickly. The beef stock recipe in this book takes only a few hours.

Follow these tips for making a good stock:

- Start with cool water. Never add ingredients to warm water.

- Bring the pot to a slow simmer. If you boil the stock, it will become cloudy.

- Never stir stock. You want the ingredients to fall or rise to the top of the pot naturally.

- Do not cover stock, as the lid will allow the steam to form water droplets that will fall back into the stock and stir it up again.

Store stock in an airtight container in the refrigerator for up to 3 days or in the freezer for up to 4 months. You can divide it among several smaller containers, such as 2-cup (1-pint) sealed jars, then store in the freezer and grab only what you need.

CHICKEN STOCK

Chicken stock can be used for just about any dish. This recipe uses a whole 4-pound chicken, but if you have access to a chicken carcass, use about 5 pounds of bones. If using the whole chicken, cook it in the liquid for 1 hour, then remove and let cool, strip the meat, and put the bones back in the liquid to simmer for another hour. **MAKES 4 QUARTS**

PREP TIME: 15 minutes | **COOK TIME:** 2 hours 15 minutes

1 (4-pound) whole
   chicken, rinsed and liver
   removed, or 5-pound
   chicken carcass
½ tablespoon whole
   black peppercorns
1 bay leaf
6 garlic cloves, halved
½ bunch fresh parsley
2 medium onions, skin
   on, quartered
4 or 5 celery stalks,
   cut into large pieces
   (about 2 cups)
4 or 5 carrots, cut
   into large pieces
   (about 2 cups)
4 quarts cool water

1. In an 8-quart stockpot, place the chicken with the neck, heart, and gizzard.

2. Add the peppercorns, bay leaf, garlic, parsley, onions, celery, and carrots. Add the water. Bring to a strong simmer, then immediately reduce the heat to a slow simmer. Cook, uncovered, for 1 hour.

3. Using a slotted spoon or tongs, remove the chicken from the liquid and let cool. Remove and discard the skin, then remove the meat from the bones. (Reserve the meat for another use, such as chicken gumbo or chicken salad.) Put the bones back in the pot and simmer for 1 more hour.

4. Skim and discard any fat at the top of the stock.

5. Line a strainer with cheesecloth, and strain the stock into a large pot or bowl. Allow the stock to drip for several minutes. Discard the bones and vegetables.

6. Let cool, then store in an airtight container in the refrigerator for up to 3 days or in the freezer for up to 4 months.

STORAGE TIP: You can store the stock in one large container or several 1-pint containers so you can grab only what you need.

BEEF STOCK

Beef stock is essential for any beef or hearty sauce, gravy, or soup. It also adds great flavor to gumbo. This simple one-pot stock uses beef bones and typical stock ingredients, but it simmers for only 4 hours because the beef bones are cut in pieces and release the flavor much more quickly. (Larger bones take longer.) The recipe requires more water than the other stocks because the longer cooking time causes more liquid to evaporate. **MAKES 4 QUARTS**

PREP TIME: 15 minutes | **COOK TIME:** 4 hours 15 minutes

8 pounds beef bones, sawed into 2- to 4-inch pieces

½ tablespoon whole black peppercorns

1 bay leaf

6 garlic cloves, halved

½ bunch fresh parsley

2 medium onions, skin on, quartered

4 or 5 celery stalks, cut into large pieces (about 2 cups)

4 or 5 carrots, cut into large pieces (about 2 cups)

6 quarts cool water

1. In a 10-quart stockpot, place the beef bones, peppercorns, bay leaf, garlic, parsley, onions, celery, and carrots. Add the water. Bring to a running simmer, then reduce the heat to a slow simmer. Cook, uncovered, for at least 4 hours (longer if you have time).

2. Skim and discard any foam and fat at the top of the stock.

3. Line a strainer with cheesecloth and strain the stock into a large pot or bowl. Allow the stock to drip for several minutes. Discard the bones and vegetables.

4. Let cool, then store in an airtight container in the refrigerator for up to 3 days or in the freezer for up to 4 months.

STORAGE TIP: You can store the stock in one large container or several 1-pint containers so you can grab only what you need.

PREPARATION TIP: Traditionally beef stocks are simmered for 12 or more hours, but cutting the bones allows you to shorten the cook time.

VEGETABLE STOCK

ONE POT, VEGETARIAN

A vegetable stock is a great alternative for vegan or vegetarian recipes. Any vegetable dish that calls for water is greatly enhanced by using vegetable stock in its place. **MAKES 4 QUARTS**

PREP TIME: 25 minutes | **COOK TIME:** 2 hours 15 minutes

½ tablespoon whole black peppercorns

1 bay leaf

6 garlic cloves, halved

½ bunch fresh parsley

1 bunch scallions, chopped

2 medium onions, skin on, quartered

4 or 5 celery stalks, cut into large pieces (about 2 cups)

4 or 5 carrots, cut into large pieces (about 2 cups)

8 ounces cabbage, chopped (about 2 cups)

2 large tomatoes, quartered

4 quarts cool water

1. In an 8-quart stockpot, place the peppercorns, bay leaf, garlic, parsley, scallions, onions, celery, carrots, cabbage, and tomatoes. Add the water. Bring to a running simmer, then reduce the heat to a slow simmer. Cook, uncovered, for 2 hours.

2. Skim and discard any foam and fat at the top of the stock.

3. Line a strainer with cheesecloth, and strain the stock into a large pot or bowl. Allow the stock to drip for several minutes. Discard the vegetables.

4. Let cool, then store in an airtight container in the refrigerator for up to 3 days or in the freezer for up to 4 months.

STORAGE TIP: You can store the stock in one large container or several 1-pint containers so you can grab only what you need.

SUBSTITUTION TIP: You can add any other vegetables, including eggplant, mushrooms, corncobs, bell peppers, chard, fresh herbs, greens, carrot tops, beet tops, radish tops, broccoli bottoms, and cauliflower cores.

SEAFOOD STOCK

ONE POT

You can make seafood stock with the bones and heads of any freshwater or saltwater fish, including trout, cod, red snapper, pollock, haddock, perch, bass, tuna, flounder, and salmon, or any crustacean shells, such as shrimp, crabs, and lobster. For a truly rich seafood stock, use a mix of bones, heads, and shells. MAKES 4 quarts

PREP TIME: 15 minutes | **COOK TIME:** 1 hour 20 minutes

2 pounds fish bones and heads; shrimp, crab, or lobster shells; or a mix

1 cup white wine

½ tablespoon whole black peppercorns

1 bay leaf

6 garlic cloves, halved

½ bunch fresh parsley

2 medium onions, skin on, quartered

4 or 5 celery stalks, cut into large pieces (about 2 cups)

4 or 5 carrots, cut into large pieces (about 2 cups)

4 quarts cool water

1. In an 8-quart stockpot, place the fish bones and heads and seafood shells. Add the white wine. Bring to a low simmer, gently stir the bones and shells, and let the wine cook through the bones for 3 to 4 minutes.

2. Add the peppercorns, bay leaf, garlic, parsley, onions, celery, and carrots. Add the water. Bring to a running simmer, then reduce the heat to a low simmer. Cook, uncovered, for 1 hour.

3. Skim and discard any foam and fat at the top of the stock.

4. Line a strainer with cheesecloth, and strain the stock into a large pot or bowl. Allow the stock to drip for several minutes. Discard the bones, heads, shells, and vegetables.

5. Let cool, then store in an airtight container in the refrigerator for up to 3 days or in the freezer for up to 4 months.

STORAGE TIP: You can store the stock in one large container or several 1-pint containers so you can grab only what you need.

SPICE BLENDS

Store-bought seasonings tend to sit in the pantry for months or even years, losing their pungency, flavor, and aroma. Making small batches of your own spice blends allows you to experiment with different flavor combinations and control the quality and shelf life. I use the following three spice blends most: Cajun spice blend is my all-around seasoning when I want a boost of flavor or for any highly spiced Cajun and Creole dishes; grill barbecue rub is perfect for grilling or roasting large cuts of meat or burgers and boneless chicken breasts; and I add Creole spice blend to gumbos, jamba-laya, and many other recipes.

The common ingredients are ground pepper, onion powder, garlic powder, and salt. Mix up your spice blends and store them in the pantry. When you're cooking, grab the one you need, measure it out, and add it to the dish. No need to measure out 10 spices for each recipe—just make the spice blend once and you're set for a couple of months.

Be sure to keep your spice blends in airtight containers and store them in a cool, dry, draft-free location away from sunlight. Moisture, light, and heat will break down and destroy their delicate flavors.

CAJUN SPICE BLEND

30 MINUTES, DAIRY-FREE, ONE POT, VEGETARIAN

This blend works great for all the recipes in this book that call for it—and there are a lot! The trio of cayenne pepper, black pepper, and white pepper, combined with garlic powder, onion powder, and dry mustard, gives this seasoning the distinctive heat and flavor found in many Cajun dishes. **MAKES ¼ CUP**

PREP TIME: 10 minutes

½ tablespoon
   cayenne pepper
½ tablespoon freshly
   ground black pepper
½ tablespoon
   white pepper
½ tablespoon
   garlic powder
½ tablespoon
   onion powder
½ tablespoon dry mustard
2 tablespoons kosher salt

In a medium bowl, combine the cayenne pepper, black pepper, white pepper, garlic powder, onion powder, dry mustard, and salt and stir until well mixed.

STORAGE TIP: Store in an airtight container or a mason jar with a screw-top lid. This blend will keep for several months in the pantry. Feel free to double or triple the recipe if you plan on using more than ¼ cup within 2 months.

PREPARATION TIP: For a finer consistency, put all the ingredients in a food processor and pulse for a few seconds. Doing so also helps blend everything nicely.

GRILL BARBECUE RUB

30 MINUTES, DAIRY-FREE, ONE POT, VEGETARIAN

This recipe was inspired by an old Memphis-style rub I perfected a long time ago. I've modified it a bit over the years, but it still captures the same smoky richness I've always loved. The smoked paprika flavor is a perfect match for dark brown and white sugars. I use this blend for all my barbecues and roasts. It's great with pork ribs, roasted chicken and turkey, hamburgers, pork shoulder roasts, pork loins, and chicken pieces. I even put it on popcorn and toss it around in a big bowl. **MAKES ½ CUP**

PREP TIME: 10 minutes

½ tablespoon chili powder

½ tablespoon
  onion powder

½ tablespoon
  garlic powder

½ tablespoon celery seed

½ tablespoon
  ground cumin

½ tablespoon freshly
  ground black pepper

1 tablespoon
  smoked paprika

1 tablespoon dried thyme

2 tablespoons dark
  brown sugar

2 tablespoons
  granulated sugar

1 tablespoon kosher salt

In a medium bowl, combine the chili powder, onion powder, garlic powder, celery seed, ground cumin, black pepper, smoked paprika, thyme, brown sugar, granulated sugar, and salt and stir until well mixed. If the sugar starts to clump, put all the ingredients in the food processor and pulse for several seconds to blend the spices and remove the lumps.

STORAGE TIP: Store in an airtight container or a mason jar with a screw-top lid. The rub will keep for several months in the pantry. Feel free to double or triple the recipe if you plan on using more than ¼ cup within two months.

PREPARATION TIP: Experiment with the recipe to suit your tastes. Try adding more sugar to enhance the sweetness or more black pepper if you want it spicier. If you'd like more salt, double the amount or add garlic salt. Celery salt might be the perfect complement for your palate. Keep a log of what you add, subtract, and modify, and note which combinations you like best.

CREOLE SPICE BLEND

30 MINUTES, DAIRY-FREE, ONE POT, VEGETARIAN

This spice blend is the indispensable seasoning used in classic Creole dishes such as gumbo, étouffée, and jambalaya as well as many recipes in this cookbook. It's a combination of black pepper, cayenne pepper, garlic powder, onion powder, basil, oregano, rosemary, thyme, dry mustard, paprika, and kosher salt. You should have it on hand at all times. **MAKES ½ CUP**

PREP TIME: 10 minutes

½ tablespoon freshly ground black pepper

½ tablespoon cayenne pepper

½ tablespoon garlic powder

½ tablespoon onion powder

½ tablespoon dried basil

½ tablespoon dried oregano

½ tablespoon dried rosemary

½ tablespoon dried thyme

½ tablespoon dry mustard

1 tablespoon paprika

1 tablespoon kosher salt

In a medium bowl, combine the black pepper, cayenne pepper, garlic powder, onion powder, basil, oregano, rosemary, thyme, dry mustard, paprika, and salt and stir until well mixed.

STORAGE TIP: Store in an airtight container or a mason jar with a screw-top lid. The blend will keep for several months in the pantry. Feel free to double or triple the recipe if you plan on using more than ¼ cup within 2 months.

ADDITIONAL ITEMS

You need a few more things for a well-stocked Cajun and Creole pantry, including the Cajun Trinity mixture of onions, celery, and bell peppers, which is included in many recipes in this book. I've also included my own flavorful version of Cocktail Sauce, a perfect accompaniment to boiled seafood. Most Cajuns love it with raw oysters or boiled shrimp.

CAJUN TRINITY

30 MINUTES, DAIRY-FREE, ONE POT, VEGETARIAN

Typically comprising equal parts chopped onions, celery, and green bell peppers, the Cajun Trinity is an integral part of many Cajun and Creole recipes. You'll find it in gumbos, étouffée, sauce piquantes, jambalayas, and a host of other dishes. Some variations call for adding chopped fresh parsley or garlic, but for the most part you'll be using the iconic trio. **MAKES 3 CUPS**

PREP TIME: 10 minutes

1 cup chopped onion

1 cup chopped celery

1 cup chopped green
   bell pepper

Mix together the onions, celery, and bell peppers and store in an airtight container in the refrigerator for up to 4 days or in the freezer for up to 3 months. When you're ready, grab what you need and sauté for about 10 minutes, depending on the recipe.

STORAGE TIP: Make larger batches of the Cajun Trinity and divide it into portions. Store in the refrigerator for up to 4 days or in the freezer for up to 4 months.

INGREDIENT TIP: The Cajun Trinity is a cousin of the French mirepoix, which is two parts onion, one part celery, and one part carrots. Mirepoix is typically used to enhance flavor and is removed or strained out before serving. The Cajun Trinity, on the other hand, is kept in the preparation as an integral part of the dish.

COCKTAIL SAUCE

30 MINUTES, DAIRY-FREE, ONE POT, VEGETARIAN

I typically throw together cocktail sauce at the last minute before we sit down to a mess of boiled shrimp, freshly shucked oysters, or fried seafood. I usually just eyeball the measurements because the amount changes depending on how many people we have at the house. This recipe makes a small batch, but you can double or triple it if you're hosting a large gathering. **MAKES 2½ CUPS**

PREP TIME: 10 minutes

½ tablespoon hot sauce (I
  like Crystal Hot Sauce)
½ tablespoon
  Worcestershire sauce
1 tablespoon freshly
  squeezed lemon juice
1½ tablespoons
  prepared horseradish
1 cup ketchup
1 cup tomato-based
  chili sauce

In a medium bowl, combine the hot sauce, Worcestershire sauce, lemon juice, horseradish, ketchup, and chili sauce and stir until well mixed. Transfer to a bowl and serve immediately.

STORAGE TIP: If you want to make this sauce ahead of time, store in an airtight container in the refrigerator for up to 5 days.

INGREDIENT TIP: If the amount of horseradish is too much for your liking, add more ketchup to offset the heat.

CHAPTER 3

SMALL PLATES AND APPETIZERS

Appetizers are all about presentation. You can start a dinner, celebration, or party with individual plates for a formal sit-down meal or on platters for a more relaxed setting. This chapter shares several of my favorite small plates and appetizers, including Jalapeño Poppers, crabmeat-filled Avocado Boats, a fun variation on the classic Black-and-Blue Chicken sandwich, spicy Deviled Eggs, and breaded Boudin Sausage Balls with mustard dipping sauce. No matter how you serve them, these starters will kick off your celebration with a bang.

Crawfish Cucumber Imperial, page 35

CRAWFISH CAKES

30 MINUTES, DAIRY-FREE

These cakes are similar to traditional crab cakes but substitute crawfish tail meat, which is typically less expensive than lump crabmeat. Sautéing the Cajun Trinity with the Cajun Spice Blend releases flavor and reduces the crunch. Of the many hot sauce brands on the market, my favorite is the New Orleans homegrown brand Crystal Hot Sauce. **MAKES 8 CAKES**

PREP TIME: 20 minutes | **COOK TIME:** 10 minutes

2 tablespoons unsalted butter, divided

1 cup Cajun Trinity (page 24)

1 tablespoon Cajun Spice Blend (page 20)

2 tablespoons minced garlic

¼ cup chopped scallions

1 pound crawfish tail meat

2 tablespoons Creole mustard (I like Zatarain's), plus more for serving

1 tablespoon Worcestershire sauce

1 tablespoon hot sauce (I like Crystal Hot Sauce)

1 tablespoon freshly squeezed lemon juice

¼ cup mayonnaise

1 large egg, beaten

1½ cups Italian bread crumbs, divided

1. In a medium sauté pan, melt 1 tablespoon of unsalted butter over medium heat. Add the Cajun Trinity and Cajun spice blend and cook, stirring, until soft and translucent, about 5 minutes. Stir in the garlic and scallions and cook for about 2 more minutes, just to release some of the garlic flavor. Remove from the heat and let cool to room temperature.

2. In a medium bowl, combine the crawfish, Creole mustard, Worcestershire sauce, hot sauce, lemon juice, mayonnaise, egg, and ½ cup of bread crumbs. Add the Cajun Trinity and stir well to combine.

3. Divide the mixture into 8 equal portions and form them into round 1-inch-thick cakes. Gently roll the cakes in the remaining 1 cup of bread crumbs.

4. In a medium sauté pan, melt the remaining 1 tablespoon of butter over medium heat. Cook the cakes in two batches of four for 3 to 4 minutes on each side, or until brown. Serve immediately with a side of Creole mustard.

STORAGE TIP: If you want to start this recipe ahead of time, stop at the end of step 2, cover the mixture, and refrigerate for up to 2 days. You can also shape the cakes, coat them in the bread crumbs, cover, and refrigerate for up to 2 days. Either way, pick up at step 3.

PREPARATION TIP: If you want to try a slightly lighter version, eliminate the butter and bake the crawfish cakes instead. Preheat the oven to 425°F. Coat a baking sheet with nonstick spray and space the crawfish cakes evenly on the sheet. Bake for 10 minutes, flip, and bake for 10 more minutes, or until browned.

JALAPEÑO POPPERS

One of my favorite hot appetizers, these poppers are delicious, quick, and easy to prepare in a single, small baking sheet. The large shrimp are tossed with Grill Barbecue Rub before being stuffed into the jalapeños with the cream cheese mixture. Add a water chestnut, wrap the whole thing in a slice of bacon, and voilà. You can cook the poppers in the oven or grill over indirect heat until the bacon is crispy. **MAKES 16 POPPERS**

PREP TIME: 25 minutes | **COOK TIME:** 30 minutes

8 fresh jalapeños, sliced
   lengthwise and seeded

16 shrimp, peeled
   and deveined

1 tablespoon Grill
   Barbecue Rub plus
   ½ tablespoon (page 21)

8 ounces cream
   cheese, softened

4 ounces shredded
   Colby cheese

1 can water
   chestnuts, drained

1 pound bacon, sliced

1. Place the jalapeños on a baking sheet and set aside.

2. Coat the shrimp with 1 tablespoon of barbecue rub and toss well, then set aside.

3. Preheat the oven to 375°F or turn on one side of your grill for indirect heat.

4. Place the cream cheese in a medium bowl. Fold in the Colby cheese and remaining ½ tablespoon of barbecue rub until fully incorporated.

5. Stuff the jalapeños with the cheese mixture, then top each with 1 water chestnut and 1 shrimp. Stretch out a slice of bacon, then wrap it around one stuffed jalapeño. Repeat with the remaining bacon and jalapeños.

6. Place in the oven or on the grill. Cook for 30 minutes, or until the bacon is crispy. Transfer to a platter and serve immediately.

SIMPLIFY IT: You can prepare the jalapeño poppers ahead of time through the bacon-wrap step, then cover the baking sheet with plastic wrap or aluminum foil and store in the refrigerator for up to 2 days.

CREOLE SALSA

30 MINUTES, DAIRY-FREE, VEGETARIAN

This chunky salsa offers mild heat with the addition of green chiles. **MAKES 4 CUPS**

PREP TIME: 20 minutes

1 bunch cilantro leaves, coarsely chopped

8 garlic cloves

½ tablespoon Creole Spice Blend (page 22)

½ tablespoon Worcestershire sauce

Juice of 1 lime

1 teaspoon garlic salt

1 tablespoon olive oil

2 jalapeño peppers, sliced

½ cup chopped scallions

1 medium red onion, cut into large chunks

4 Roma tomatoes, cut into large chunks

1 (4½-ounce) can diced green chiles

1 cup crushed tomatoes

1 cup tomato-based chili sauce

1. Place the cilantro and garlic in a food processor and finely chop.

2. Add the Creole spice blend, Worcestershire sauce, lime juice, garlic salt, olive oil, jalapeños, scallions, red onions, tomatoes, and green chiles. Pulse several times, until the tomatoes and onion are coarsely chopped and all the ingredients are well mixed.

3. Transfer the mixture to a large bowl, then add the crushed tomatoes and chili sauce. Stir well to incorporate.

4. Transfer the salsa to a bowl and serve with tortilla chips, vegetable chips, or your favorite dipper.

STORAGE TIP: Store in an airtight container in the refrigerator for up to 5 days. (It has never lasted that long in our house!)

INGREDIENT TIP: This salsa is perfect as a chilled dip, but it's also great heated up and served warm as a sauce, particularly over fried or poached eggs or grilled tuna or swordfish.

AVOCADO BOATS WITH CRABMEAT AND CREOLE SALSA

30 MINUTES, DAIRY-FREE, ONE POT

This appetizer is quick and easy to put together with fresh avocados, lump crabmeat, and a sprinkling of Cajun Spice Blend. It's an adaptation of an entrée-size recipe of halved avocados topped with crabmeat stuffing and freshly grated Parmesan cheese, baked in the oven, and served piping hot. **MAKES 16 BOATS**

PREP TIME: 10 minutes

4 avocados

½ pound lump crabmeat

½ cup Creole Salsa
   (page 31)

1 tablespoon Cajun Spice
   Blend (page 20)

1. Cut each avocado in half lengthwise, remove the pit, and cut each half lengthwise again. Repeat with the remaining avocados until you have 16 avocado boats.

2. Place 1 tablespoon of crabmeat in the center of each avocado boat, then top with ½ tablespoon of Creole salsa. Arrange the boats on a serving platter and sprinkle evenly with the Cajun spice blend. Serve immediately.

PREPARATION TIP: You cannot make these ahead of time, but if you do need to prep them before serving, sprinkle a bit of fresh lemon juice over the avocado. Doing so will help prevent oxidizing, which makes the avocado turn brown and mushy.

BLACK-AND-BLUE CHICKEN ON BASIL TOAST

30 MINUTES

This dish was originally served as a sandwich called Blackened and Blue Chicken at the City Energy Club (CEC) in New Orleans in the 1990s. This appetizer version replaces the original bun with French bread toast rounds and adds fresh basil paste. **SERVES 16**

PREP TIME: 15 minutes | **COOK TIME:** 15 minutes

FOR THE SANDWICHES

1 loaf French bread, cut into 1-inch rounds

1½ pounds boneless, skinless chicken breasts

2 tablespoons olive oil

1 tablespoon Cajun Spice Blend (page 20)

1 cup basil paste

½ cup store-bought blue cheese dressing

TO MAKE THE SANDWICHES

1. Place the bread on a baking sheet and set aside. Place a large cast-iron skillet over high heat and let it get hot.

2. Slice the chicken breasts in half lengthwise to get two thin pieces each. Brush them all over with the olive oil, then lightly sprinkle them with the Cajun spice blend.

3. Working in batches, place four pieces of chicken in the skillet and cook for 5 to 6 minutes, or until the edges turn opaque or white. Flip and cook for 5 more minutes. Transfer the cooked chicken to a platter. Repeat with the remaining chicken. Let sit at least 5 minutes, then cut into ½-inch-thick slices. Keep the skillet over high heat.

4. Using a rubber spatula, coat both sides of the bread with the basil paste. Working in batches, place the bread in the hot skillet and cook for 2 to 3 minutes on each side, or until brown and crusty. Repeat with the remaining bread.

5. Transfer the bread to a serving platter. Place several pieces of the chicken on each slice of bread. Top with 1 teaspoon of blue cheese dressing. Serve immediately.

INGREDIENTS CONTINUED >

CONTINUED >

FOR THE BASIL PASTE

2 cups fresh basil leaves

¼ cup minced garlic

1 cup olive oil

½ cup freshly shredded
  Parmesan cheese

1 teaspoon Cajun Spice
  Blend (page 20)

TO MAKE THE BASIL PASTE

Place the basil, garlic, olive oil, Parmesan cheese, and Cajun spice blend in a food processor and pulse until the mixture has a smooth paste consistency. Use immediately. Store leftovers in an airtight container in the refrigerator for up to 5 days.

INGREDIENT TIP: You can season the chicken and marinate it ahead of time. Store in the refrigerator in an airtight container for several hours or overnight.

CRAWFISH CUCUMBER IMPERIAL

30 MINUTES

This cold appetizer, which can be prepared several hours in advance of serving, is a perfect way to enjoy crawfish tails in a spicy salad on a cucumber round. You can use jumbo lump crabmeat instead of crawfish or shrimp. I prefer Zatarain's Creole mustard because of its unique and vibrant flavor. **SERVES 16**

PREP TIME: 15 minutes

Parchment paper

2 large cucumbers, cut into 1-inch-thick rounds

1 pound crawfish tail meat or 1 pound medium-size shrimp, boiled and chilled

1 tablespoon Creole mustard (I like Zatarain's)

1 tablespoon Cajun Spice Blend (page 20)

¼ cup chopped fresh parsley

½ cup mayonnaise

2 scallions, chopped

1 cup Cajun Trinity, finely diced (page 24)

Parsley sprigs, for garnish (optional)

Grape tomato wedges, for garnish (optional)

1. Line a baking sheet with parchment paper or plastic wrap. Using a melon baller or a teaspoon, scoop out a well from each cucumber round without cutting through the bottom. Place the rounds on the prepared baking sheet and set aside.

2. In a medium bowl, combine the crawfish, Creole mustard, Cajun spice blend, parsley, mayonnaise, scallions, and Cajun Trinity and stir well.

3. Top each cucumber round with about 1 tablespoon of crawfish salad. Transfer to a cold platter, garnish with parsley sprigs and tomato wedges (if using), and serve immediately.

STORAGE TIP: You can make the filling ahead of time and store it in a covered bowl in the refrigerator for several hours, or until ready to stuff the cucumbers. You can also prepare the entire dish and store on a baking sheet in the refrigerator for up to 8 hours.

PREPARATION TIP: If you don't like a wet filling, drain the crawfish or shrimp in a colander for 10 minutes before mixing with the other ingredients.

DEVILED EGGS

30 MINUTES

Cajun spice adds tang to these deviled eggs, but it's balanced with the cream cheese and mayonnaise. The filling is piped into the boiled egg whites from a pastry bag fitted with a large star tip and topped with olives and a dash of paprika. Always a treat on the holidays, these deviled eggs are also the perfect finger food for any occasion. **MAKES 12 DEVILED EGGS**

PREP TIME: 15 minutes | **COOK TIME:** 15 minutes

6 large eggs

3 cups ice water bath

1 teaspoon Cajun Spice Blend (page 20)

1 tablespoon Creole mustard (I like Zatarain's)

1 tablespoon sweet pickle relish

¼ cup mayonnaise

4 ounces cream cheese, softened

6 queen olives, cut in half horizontally

½ teaspoon paprika

1. Place the eggs in a large saucepan and cover with cool water. Bring to a boil over high heat and cook for 10 minutes. Set up the ice water bath.

2. Drain the hot water, then gently place the eggs in the ice water bath. Let sit until completely cooled, about 10 minutes.

3. Peel the eggs, then cut them in half lengthwise. Remove the yolks and place them in a food processor. Place the whites on a large plate and store in the refrigerator.

4. Add the Cajun spice blend, Creole mustard, relish, mayonnaise, and cream cheese to the food processor. Process until smooth and well incorporated, ensuring no lumps remain.

5. Transfer the filling to a pastry bag fitted with a large star tip. Remove the egg whites from the refrigerator. Pipe the filling into each egg white, creating a nice circular pattern.

6. Place one olive round on the center of each egg, then lightly dust paprika over the top before serving.

SIMPLIFY IT: You can make this a day ahead. Store leftovers in the refrigerator, covered, for up to 3 days.

RED, WHITE, AND BLUE HUMMUS

30 MINUTES, DAIRY-FREE, GLUTEN-FREE, VEGETARIAN

Red kidney beans, white cannelloni beans, and blue corn chips come together in a flash to create this easy, delicious hummus. With Creole Spice Blend, it's almost like fireworks on your palate. **MAKES 4 CUPS**

PREP TIME: 10 minutes

1 (15½-ounce) can red
kidney beans

1 (15½-ounce) can white
cannelloni beans

1 tablespoon minced garlic

1 tablespoon Creole Spice
Blend (page 22)

¼ cup freshly squeezed
lemon juice

½ cup tahini

1 bag blue corn chips

1. Strain the kidney and cannelloni beans over one container. Reserve 1 cup of the mixed liquid.

2. Put the kidney and cannelloni beans, reserved liquid, garlic, Creole spice blend, lemon juice, and tahini in a food processor and blend until smooth and creamy.

3. Transfer to a serving platter and serve immediately with the blue corn chips. Store in an airtight container in the refrigerator for up to 5 days.

SUBSTITUTION TIP: Instead of blue corn chips, you can serve this hummus with vegetable chips or fresh vegetables such as cucumber slices, carrot sticks, celery sticks, broccoli or cauliflower florets, or grape tomatoes.

BOUDIN SAUSAGE BALLS

30 MINUTES

Boudin sausage balls are coated, breaded, and deep fried or roasted in the oven, and served with Creole mustard. *Boudin* means sausage in French. Cajun boudin is typically a white sausage, or *boudin blanc*, that consists of pork meat, pork liver, white rice, the Cajun Trinity, and a variety of spices stuffed into hog casing. Boudin is hard to find outside Louisiana, but you can order it online (see Resources, page 88) or make your own. The recipe I've included here will add about 90 minutes to your prep and cook times than if you use store-bought. **MAKES 20 SAUSAGE BALLS**

PREP TIME: 10 minutes | **COOK TIME:** 10 minutes

FOR THE SAUSAGE BALLS

½ teaspoon hot sauce (I like Crystal Hot Sauce)

½ tablespoon Cajun Spice Blend (page 20)

2 tablespoons cool water

2 large eggs, lightly beaten

1½ cups Italian bread crumbs

1½ pounds raw boudin, removed from the casing

2 quarts peanut oil

1 cup Creole mustard (I like Zatarain's)

TO MAKE THE SAUSAGE BALLS

1. In a medium bowl, whisk together the hot sauce, Cajun spice blend, cool water, and eggs. Place the bread crumbs in another medium bowl. Roll the boudin into 20 ping-pong-size balls, about 1 ounce each.

2. In a large stock pot or Dutch oven, heat the peanut oil over medium heat until a deep fryer thermometer reads 350°F.

3. Dip each boudin ball in the egg mixture, then roll in the bread crumbs, coating evenly. Fry the balls in small batches (about 5 per batch) for 3 to 4 minutes each, or until light brown.

4. Drain on a plate lined with paper towels, transfer to a serving platter, and serve immediately with the Creole mustard.

FOR THE BOUDIN

2 cups cool water

1 teaspoon kosher salt

1 cup short-grain rice

1 pound pork shoulder, cut
into 1-inch cubes

½ pound pork liver, cut
into 1-inch cubes

1 quart water

1½ cups Cajun
Trinity (page 24),
coarsely chopped

1 tablespoon Cajun Spice
Blend (page 20)

4 tablespoons chopped
fresh parsley
leaves, divided

4 tablespoons chopped
scallions, divided

TO MAKE THE BOUDIN

1. In a small saucepan, bring the water and salt to a boil. Add the rice, reduce the heat to low, and simmer for about 20 minutes, or until the rice is cooked. Transfer the rice to a large bowl and let cool.

2. In a large 3-quart stock pot, place the pork shoulder, pork liver, water, Cajun Trinity, Cajun spice blend, 2 tablespoons of parsley, and 2 tablespoons of scallions. Bring to a boil, then reduce the heat to a simmer and cook for about 1 hour, or until the pork shoulder and liver are tender. Remove from the heat and drain the liquid, reserving about 1 cup.

3. Transfer the mixture, plus the remaining 2 tablespoons of parsley and 2 tablespoons of scallions, to a food processor. Pulse until coarsely chopped. Transfer to the bowl of rice and mix well.

4. Mix in the reserved liquid, about 1/3 cup at a time, until the boudin is moist and holds together when squeezed.

STORAGE TIP: If making your own boudin, you can roll out the balls and store in an airtight container in the refrigerator for several days or in the freezer for up to 4 months.

INGREDIENT TIP: If you don't like pork liver, substitute ½ pound of pork shoulder.

CHAPTER 4

CLASSIC CAJUN AND CREOLE MAINS

Cajun and Creole recipes cook best in big pots, and most of the recipes in this chapter require only one. I've included a few soups, like Crawfish Bisque, New Orleans Seafood Chowder, and Oyster Artichoke Soup as well as Blackened Fish, the dish Paul Prudhomme made famous. You'll also find Pecan-Crusted Chicken Breasts with Cajun Artichoke Beurre Blanc, Turkey Creole Skillet, Smothered Pork Chops, Shrimp Stuffed Bell Peppers, Honey and Creole Mustard-Glazed Salmon, and more. These dishes will have everyone at the table clamoring for seconds.

Coq au Vin, page 47

SHRIMP AND OKRA GUMBO

DAIRY-FREE, ONE POT

There must be as many variations of gumbo as there are folks who make their own. This version uses the traditional shrimp and okra base. The gumbo filé powder is mixed with a little cool water to form a slurry, which keeps the powder from forming clumps. You can modify the recipe to add any protein, depending on the season and availability, such as andouille sausage, Tasso ham, chicken, oysters, and even duck. **SERVES 8**

PREP TIME: 20 minutes | **COOK TIME:** 45 minutes

½ cup Dark Roux
(page 13)

1½ cups Cajun Trinity,
diced large (page 24)

½ tablespoon Creole
Spice Blend (page 22)

1 tablespoon
minced garlic

64 ounces (½ gallon)
Chicken Stock (page 15)

1 cup diced tomatoes

1 bay leaf

1 tablespoon
Worcestershire sauce

½ tablespoon hot sauce
(I like Crystal Hot Sauce)

½ pound okra, sliced
½-inch thick

1 tablespoon gumbo
filé powder

¼ cup cool water

1. In a 4-quart stockpot, cook the dark roux over medium heat until it just starts to bubble. Add the Cajun Trinity and Creole spice blend, and cook, stirring well, until softened.

2. Add the garlic and continue to cook for a few minutes. Add the chicken stock, tomatoes, bay leaf, Worcestershire sauce, and hot sauce, and bring to a boil. Reduce the heat to a simmer. Add the okra and stir well. Bring back to a simmer until the okra is cooked.

3. In a small mixing bowl, combine the gumbo filé powder and cool water and whisk into a slurry, until the powder has dissolved. Fold the slurry into the gumbo. Simmer for a few more minutes, until well incorporated.

½ pound shrimp, 21 to
   30 count

1 cup diced scallions

Kosher salt

White pepper

Steamed white rice,
   for serving

4. Gently fold in the shrimp and scallions and simmer for 5 minutes, until the shrimp are pink and heated through. Season with salt and white pepper to taste. To serve, ladle 1 cup per serving in large soup bowls along with the steamed white rice.

SUBSTITUTION TIP: If you want to add sausage or Tasso ham, slice or dice it, cook down a few minutes, and add with the Cajun Trinity (page 24) in step 1. If you want to add chicken or duck, roast about 1 pound, let cool, peel off the skin, remove the meat from the bone, cube the meat, and add with the shrimp in step 4. Add raw oysters with the shrimp in step 4.

BLACKENED FISH

30 MINUTES, DAIRY-FREE, GLUTEN-FREE

To get a really good blackening on your fish, use a very hot cast-iron skillet or griddle. But beware: Blackening in a skillet can produce a lot of smoke. Countless times I've set off the alarm! Unless you have a very good vent hood exhaust system in your kitchen, it's best to use your outdoor grill to get the heat you want for this recipe. **SERVES 4**

PREP TIME: 10 minutes | **COOK TIME:** 10 minutes

4 (4- to 6-ounce) catfish fillets

½ cup peanut oil

2 tablespoons Cajun Spice Blend (page 20)

2 teaspoons garlic salt

1. Prepare the grill with about 5 pounds of charcoal and heat until the coals are white, or preheat the gas grill to high. Place a cast-iron griddle or skillet over the coals or gas burner for 20 minutes, until it is very hot.

2. Meanwhile, coat the catfish fillets with the peanut oil, then sprinkle with Cajun spice blend and garlic salt on both sides. Marinate for 20 minutes.

3. Cook for 5 minutes, until white, then flip and cook for 5 more minutes, until flaky. Serve immediately.

SIMPLIFY IT: You can prep this recipe the night before. Combine the peanut oil and Cajun Spice Blend in a large zip-top bag, then add the catfish fillets. Seal the bag tightly, toss the catfish in the mixture, and marinate overnight in the refrigerator. When you're ready to cook, heat the grill and pick up with step 3.

SLOW COOKER RED BEANS

DAIRY-FREE, ONE POT

You can find red beans and rice in just about every mom-and-pop corner grocery, deli, or lunch counter in New Orleans. It's also a staple in diners, cafés, and buffet lines. Back in the day, Monday was for laundry, and because it was an arduous task without modern appliances, home cooks usually put on a big pot of red beans and let them cook slowly with little supervision. This recipe is easy to double, and it tastes even better the next day. It also freezes beautifully. **SERVES 8**

PREP TIME: 10 minutes | **COOK TIME:** 8 hours 30 minutes

1 pound red kidney beans

1 pound smoked sausage, cut into ¼-inch rounds

3 cups Cajun Trinity (page 24)

1 tablespoon minced garlic

4 cups Beef Stock (page 16)

1 tablespoon Creole Spice Blend (page 22)

1 bay leaf

1 tablespoon Worcestershire sauce

½ tablespoon hot sauce (I like Crystal Hot Sauce)

1. Set a slow cooker to the highest setting. Place the beans, sausage, Cajun Trinity, garlic, beef stock, Creole spice blend, bay leaf, Worcestershire sauce, and hot sauce in the slow cooker, stir well, and cover. Be sure there is enough stock to cover all the ingredients, and add more if needed.

2. Once the slow cooker starts to simmer, reduce the heat to low and cook for 7 hours.

3. Remove the cover and stir well. Use the back of a spoon to mash some of the beans against the inside of the slow cooker, which helps them thicken. Cook on medium-low heat for 1 more hour so the beans can thicken even more before serving.

VARIATION TIP: You can make this meal vegan by using vegan red beans, Vegetable Stock (page 17), and vegan sausage in place of the beef stock and smoked sausage.

CRAWFISH BISQUE

My in-laws handed down this recipe, which I've turned into a creamy one-pot soup. Crawfish are in peak season in May. **SERVES 8**

PREP TIME: 20 minutes | **COOK TIME:** 40 minutes

3 cups Cajun
  Trinity (page 24),
  coarsely diced
4 garlic cloves
10 parsley sprigs
1 cup Blond Roux
  (page 12)
1 tablespoon Cajun Spice
  Blend (page 20)
2 tablespoons
  tomato paste
2 quarts Seafood Stock
  (page 18)
2 pounds crawfish tail
  meat, divided
1 cup heavy cream
½ cup brandy
1 teaspoon kosher salt
¼ teaspoon
  cayenne pepper

1. Place the Cajun Trinity, garlic, and parsley in a food processor and grind until the ingredients are smooth. In a 4-quart stockpot, heat the blond roux over medium heat, stirring, until it darkens slightly. Add the garlic mixture and Cajun spice blend and cook on low heat, stirring frequently, for 10 minutes, or until the mixture is soft and the onions from the Cajun Trinity are translucent.

2. Add the tomato paste, stir, and simmer for 3 minutes.

3. Add the seafood stock and stir well, until fully incorporated into the roux mixture. Increase the heat to medium and bring to a boil, then reduce the heat to a simmer over low heat, stirring occasionally. The bisque should start to thicken as it simmers.

4. In the food processor, grind 1 pound of crawfish into a smooth paste. Add the crawfish paste to the bisque and continue to simmer. Add the heavy cream, brandy, and remaining crawfish. Stir well to incorporate. Simmer for 5 minutes, then stir in the salt and cayenne pepper. Serve in soup bowls.

INGREDIENT TIP: A loaf of warmed French bread cut into 2-inch rounds is a great accompaniment to this rich bisque.

COQ AU VIN

Coq au vin means chicken with wine, and this classic dish, with its rustic form and refined preparation, is typically served over steamed rice. Although *coq* is rooster, this version calls for boneless, skinless chicken breasts, which require less cooking time than a whole bone-in chicken. **SERVES 8**

PREP TIME: 15 minutes | **COOK TIME:** 1 hour 10 minutes

8 (4-ounce) boneless, skinless chicken breasts

1 tablespoon Cajun Spice Blend (page 20)

4 tablespoons (½ stick) butter, divided

¼ cup brandy, divided

½ pound mushrooms, sliced

1 cup diced onions

1 tablespoon minced garlic

3 tablespoons all-purpose flour

¼ cup tomato sauce

¼ cup diced pimentos

1 cup dry red wine (try Burgundy or Merlot)

1½ cups Chicken Stock (page 15)

¼ cup chopped scallions

Steamed rice, for serving

1. Season the chicken all over with Cajun spice blend. In a large sauté pan or cast-iron skillet, melt 1 tablespoon of butter over medium heat. Add four chicken breasts and cook until browned on all sides. Add 2 tablespoons of brandy and allow it to simmer. Transfer the chicken to a platter. Repeat with 1 tablespoon of butter and the remaining four chicken breasts and 2 tablespoons of brandy.

2. In the same pan, melt the remaining 2 tablespoons of butter over medium heat. Add the mushrooms and onions and cook, stirring well, until slightly browned. Add the garlic and cook, stirring, for just 1 minute. Add the flour and stir well, until mixed evenly with the mushroom and onions. Cook for about 3 minutes.

3. Add the tomato sauce, pimentos, red wine, and chicken stock. Bring the liquid to a simmer for about 5 minutes, then add the chicken, spacing it evenly in the pan. Cover and simmer for 30 minutes.

4. When the chicken is tender, transfer the chicken and sauce to a serving dish and garnish with the scallions. Serve with a side of steamed rice.

SUBSTITUTION TIP: The traditional French recipe uses pearl onions. If you want to substitute them, use 1¾ cups because they take up more space in a volume measurement.

NEW ORLEANS SEAFOOD CHOWDER

ONE POT

I created and served this recipe many times while chef at Elmwood Medical Center in Jefferson, Louisiana. The recipe, which has a base of seafood stock and tomatoes, is a variation of a Manhattan-style chowder, but it also includes chunks of catfish, large shrimp, oysters, and crab claws. **SERVES 8**

PREP TIME: 20 minutes | COOK TIME: 45 minutes

2 tablespoons
   unsalted butter

3 cups Cajun Trinity
   (page 24), diced large

1 tablespoon Cajun Spice
   Blend (page 20)

1 tablespoon tomato paste

4 cups Seafood Stock
   (page 18)

1 (8-ounce) bottle
   clam juice

1 tablespoon hot sauce
   (I like Crystal Hot Sauce)

1 tablespoon
   Worcestershire sauce

5 cups diced tomatoes

1½ cups diced small
   red potatoes

½ pound catfish
   fillets, cubed

½ pound shrimp

1 pint raw oysters

1 pound crab claws

1. In a large 4-quart stockpot, melt the butter over medium heat. Add the Cajun Trinity and Cajun spice blend and cook for 5 minutes, stirring frequently, until soft and translucent. Add the tomato paste and stir well, until evenly incorporated. Cook for about 1 minute.

2. Add the seafood stock, clam juice, hot sauce, Worcestershire sauce, tomatoes, and potatoes, and stir well. Bring to a boil, then reduce the heat to low and simmer for about 20 minutes.

3. Add the catfish, shrimp, and oysters, and simmer for 5 to 7 minutes, or until the shrimp are pink and the oysters are curled. Fold in the crab claws and cook for 1 more minute. Serve immediately in large soup bowls.

SIMPLIFY IT: If you want to save time dicing the fresh tomatoes, substitute 3 (15-ounce) cans of diced plum tomatoes.

OYSTER ARTICHOKE SOUP

ONE POT

A perennial New Orleans favorite, this soup uses reserved liquid from the oysters, called oyster liquor, as do most recipes that call for oysters, such as oyster stew, oyster gumbo, and oysters in cream sauce. Artichoke hearts, seafood stock, heavy cream, and a blond roux make the soup rich. **SERVES 8**

PREP TIME: 15 minutes | **COOK TIME:** 35 minutes

8 tablespoons (1 stick)
  unsalted butter

3 cups Cajun Trinity
  (page 24)

1 tablespoon Cajun Spice
  Blend (page 20)

¼ cup minced garlic

1 cup chopped
  scallions, divided

½ cup all-purpose flour

3 cans artichoke hearts,
  drained, divided

3 pints raw oysters, liquor
  reserved, divided

4 cups Seafood Stock
  (page 18)

1 tablespoon
  Worcestershire sauce

2 cups heavy cream

Kosher salt

White pepper

1. In a 4-quart stockpot, melt the butter over medium heat. Add the Cajun Trinity and Cajun spice blend, stir well, and cook for 5 minutes, or until translucent. Add the garlic and ½ cup of scallions, and stir well. Cook for 2 minutes.

2. Add the flour and stir well to make a blond roux. Continue to stir and cook for 3 to 5 minutes.

3. Add 1½ cans of the artichoke hearts and 1½ pints of the oysters, stir well, and cook until the oysters are curled on the edges. Let cool a few minutes. Transfer to a food processor and blend until smooth, then transfer back to the stockpot.

4. Add the seafood stock, reserved oyster liquor, and Worcestershire sauce. Using a wire whisk, whisk into a smooth consistency. Bring to a simmer over medium heat, then add the remaining 1½ cans of artichoke hearts, remaining 1½ pints of raw oysters, and the heavy cream. Continue to simmer for 5 to 8 minutes. Add the remaining ½ cup of chopped scallions, then season with salt and white pepper to taste before serving.

INGREDIENT TIP: In step 2 you are adding the flour to make a blond roux, but if you have Blond Roux (page 12) on hand, add ½ cup instead to save a bit of time.

TURKEY CREOLE SKILLET

GLUTEN-FREE, ONE POT

This recipe was born when I was putting together a quick lunch dish of ground turkey and vegetables seasoned with Creole flavors. I added red pepper flakes for some extra heat. Sour cream will curdle if you add it directly to a hot dish, so temper it first (see the Ingredient Tip). **SERVES 4**

PREP TIME: 20 minutes | **COOK TIME:** 35 minutes

1 tablespoon
  unsalted butter

1 pound ground
  turkey meat

1 cup finely diced onions

½ pound
  mushrooms, sliced

2 cups diced tomatoes

3 cups diced eggplant

1 cup tomato-based
  chili sauce

1½ tablespoons Creole
  Spice Blend (page 22)

½ teaspoon ground ginger

½ teaspoon celery salt

4 cups fresh baby spinach

1 cup sour cream,
  tempered (see
  Ingredient Tip)

1 teaspoon red pepper
  flakes (optional)

1. In a large saucepan or cast-iron skillet, melt the butter. Add the turkey and cook until most of the pink is gone. Add the onions and cook until soft.

2. Add the mushrooms and cook until browned. Add the tomatoes, eggplant, chili sauce, Creole spice blend, ginger, and celery salt. Stir well. Cover and simmer over medium heat for 10 minutes.

3. Add the spinach and fold in until just wilted. Turn off the heat and gently fold in the tempered sour cream until incorporated.

4. To serve, portion into four bowls and add the red pepper flakes (if using).

VARIATION TIP: If you want to turn this dish into a curry, add 1 tablespoon of curry powder and 1 teaspoon of turmeric with the Creole Spice Blend in step 2.

INGREDIENT TIP: Tempering a cold ingredient gradually increases its temperature so it doesn't change composition when added to the dish. If you put the sour cream directly in the hot pan, it will curdle. To temper it, place the sour cream in a medium heatproof bowl. While the mixture is simmering in step 2, add a spoonful of the hot liquid to the sour cream and whisk to combine. Repeat twice. When you fold in the tempered sour cream, do so slowly and gently.

SHRIMP, SAUSAGE, AND GRITS

30 MINUTES

This recipe is an adaptation of the original shrimp and grits recipes you will find all along the Gulf Coast and Eastern Shore. Andouille sausage elevates the dish.. **SERVES 6**

PREP TIME: 10 minutes | **COOK TIME:** 20 minutes

4 cups Seafood Stock
(page 18)

1 cup grits (instant
or 5-minute)

½ pound Jarlsberg
cheese or Swiss cheese,
grated, divided

1 pound andouille or
smoked sausage, cut
into ½-inch cubes

4 tablespoons (½ stick)
unsalted butter

1 pound button
mushrooms, sliced

1 cup finely chopped
scallions (white and
green parts), divided

4 garlic cloves, minced

½ cup dry white wine

1 pound shrimp, peeled
and deveined

½ tablespoon Cajun Spice
Blend (page 20)

¼ cup grated
Parmesan cheese

1. In a 2-quart saucepan, bring the seafood stock to a simmer over medium heat. Stir in the grits and bring to boil, then simmer, stirring occasionally, for 5 to 7 minutes. Fold in ¼ pound or half of the Jarlsberg cheese and allow it to melt into the grits. Cover and set aside.

2. In a large sauté pan, cook the sausage on all sides over medium heat, until browned. Transfer to a plate lined with paper towels. In the same pan, melt the butter, then add the mushrooms, ¾ cup of scallions, and the garlic and cook for 3 to 4 more minutes. Add the white wine, reduce the heat, and simmer for 1 to 2 minutes. Gently add the shrimp and the Cajun spice blend and stir well.

3. Fold in the sausage and stir in the remaining ¼ pound of Jarlsberg cheese until well combined.

4. Sprinkle the remaining ¼ cup of scallions and the Parmesan cheese evenly over the top.

5. Divide the grits evenly among 6 plates, then spoon the shrimp and sausage sauce evenly over the grits. Serve immediately.

INGREDIENT TIP: After cutting the andouille sausage, pat dry the cubes with paper towels before adding them to the pan. This helps them brown quickly and more evenly.

PECAN-CRUSTED CHICKEN BREASTS WITH CAJUN ARTICHOKE BEURRE BLANC

This mouthwatering dish features goat-cheese-stuffed boneless chicken breasts coated with a pecan Cajun-spiced crust and served with zesty artichoke hearts in a creamy sauce. Beurre blanc's main ingredient is room-temperature butter, preferably unsalted. This version is made with minced shallots and a white wine reduction. It's a delicate but magnificent sauce that pairs perfectly with the pecan-crusted chicken breast. **MAKES 4 PORTIONS**

PREP TIME: 30 minutes | **COOK TIME:** 15 minutes

FOR THE CHICKEN

Plastic wrap

4 boneless
    chicken breasts

8 ounces goat cheese, cut
    into 4 even pieces

½ teaspoon kosher
    salt, plus more for
    seasoning, divided

½ teaspoon white
    pepper, plus more for
    seasoning, divided

2 cups pecan
    pieces, toasted

1 tablespoon Cajun Spice
    Blend (page 20)

2 large eggs, beaten

¼ cup milk

Parchment paper

2 cups all-purpose flour

4 tablespoons (½ stick)
    unsalted butter

TO MAKE THE CHICKEN

1. Place a layer of plastic wrap on your work surface, then lay the chicken breasts on top. Place another layer of plastic wrap over the chicken. Using a meat mallet, gently pound the chicken breasts to flatten. Remove the top layer of plastic wrap.

2. Using a boning knife, cut a slit lengthwise into a chicken breast about two-thirds of the way, creating a pocket. Repeat with the remaining chicken. Stuff 2 ounces of goat cheese into each chicken breast. Season the outside of the chicken with salt and white pepper, transfer to a baking sheet, and cover.

3. Place the pecans in a food processor and pulse until they are broken up but still a bit chunky, almost like the consistency of dry oats. Transfer to a large bowl and add the Cajun spice blend.

4. In a second large bowl, combine the beaten egg and milk.

5. In a third bowl, mix the flour, ½ teaspoon of salt, and ½ teaspoon of white pepper. Line a baking sheet with parchment paper.

FOR THE CAJUN ARTICHOKE BEURRE BLANC

½ pound (2 sticks)
unsalted butter, plus
1 tablespoon, cold

1 tablespoon
minced shallots

1½ cups artichoke hearts,
cut into quarters

1 teaspoon Cajun Spice
Blend (page 20)

½ cup white wine

1 tablespoon freshly
squeezed lemon juice

Kosher salt

White pepper

6. One at a time, dip each chicken breast into the flour mixture, shaking off excess flour. Dip into the egg mixture to coat well, letting the excess drip off. Finally, dredge in the pecan mixture, gently patting in the pecans. Set the chicken on the prepared baking sheet. Repeat with the remaining chicken breasts.

7. In a large sauté pan, melt the butter over medium heat. Cook the battered chicken breasts for 4 to 5 minutes, or until browned evenly. Flip and cook for another 3 to 4 minutes, or until golden brown on both sides. Serve immediately with beurre blanc.

TO MAKE THE CAJUN ARTICHOKE BEURRE BLANC

1. Using a small paring knife, cut ½ pound of butter into ½-inch cubes, set on a small plate, and bring to room temperature.

2. In a medium sauté pan, melt the remaining 1 tablespoon of butter. Add the shallots and cook over medium-low heat for 3 to 4 minutes, or until soft. Gently stir in the artichoke hearts and Cajun spice blend. Cook, stirring occasionally, for 3 more minutes.

3. Gently pour in the white wine and lemon juice, bring to a simmer, and reduce until almost dry, also known in French as *au sec*.

CONTINUED >

4. Remove from the heat and let cool about 5 minutes. One by one, add the room-temperature butter cubes to the pan. Stir until they smooth out but do not melt. Season with salt and white pepper to taste. Serve immediately.

SIMPLIFY IT: You can bread the chicken ahead of time and place it on a parchment-lined baking sheet. Cover with plastic wrap and refrigerate for up to 1 hour before cooking.

INGREDIENT TIP: The beurre blanc will not keep for long, as the butter will solidify in 30 to 40 minutes. To keep the sauce at the proper consistency, place it into a double boiler with a lukewarm water bath that is kept at around 76°F or room temperature.

SHRIMP AND ANDOUILLE DIRTY RICE

ONE POT

With the addition of shrimp and andouille, this dish is perfect for a rice-based main course. It also makes a great accompaniment to fried chicken, fried catfish, and grilled or blackened seafood. Don't be afraid of the chicken gizzards, which are ground up and mixed in. They add flavor but do not overpower the dish. **SERVES 6**

PREP TIME: 15 minutes | COOK TIME: 35 minutes

1½ tablespoons Creole
Spice Blend (page 22)

2 teaspoons dry mustard

2 teaspoons ground cumin

1 tablespoon
unsalted butter

½ pound ground
chicken gizzards

4 ounces ground pork

½ pound andouille
sausage, diced

1½ cups Cajun Trinity
(page 24)

4 garlic cloves, minced

2 cups Chicken Stock
(page 15)

¾ cup uncooked
converted white rice
(I like Uncle Ben's)

½ pound shrimp, peeled
and deveined

1. In a small bowl, combine the Creole spice blend, dry mustard, and cumin and set aside.

2. In a large skillet, melt the butter over medium heat. Add the chicken gizzards, pork, and sausage and cook for 5 minutes, or until the meat is browned and no pink remains. Add the spice mixture, Cajun Trinity, and garlic, and stir well. Cook for 5 more minutes, stirring frequently, until the Cajun Trinity is soft and translucent.

3. Add the chicken stock and rice, stir well, and bring to a boil. Reduce the heat to low, cover, and simmer for 15 minutes. Add the shrimp and stir well. Turn off the heat and keep the skillet on the stove, covered, for 10 more minutes, or until the rice is tender and the shrimp is pink.

4. Transfer to a casserole dish or bowl and serve immediately.

VARIATION TIP: You can use any of your favorite smoked sausages instead of the andouille, and you can replace the shrimp with crawfish tails.

SHRIMP ÉTOUFFÉE

ONE POT

This Cajun dish is perfect for 1 pound of shrimp or crawfish tail meat. At the Columns Hotel, where I worked as sous chef under Chef Chris Canan, we made a similar étouffée. Serve this étouffée over rice. **SERVES 8**

PREP TIME: 20 minutes | **COOK TIME:** 40 minutes

8 tablespoons (1 stick) unsalted butter

2 cups Cajun Trinity (page 24), diced

1 cup chopped scallions, divided

1 tablespoon minced garlic

1 bay leaf

1 tablespoon Cajun Spice Blend (page 20)

1 tablespoon chopped fresh thyme

¼ cup chopped fresh parsley

1 tablespoon paprika

1 teaspoon cayenne pepper

1 cup all-purpose flour

½ cup red wine, such as Burgundy or Merlot

½ cup white wine, such as Chardonnay

2 quarts Seafood Stock (page 18)

½ tablespoon hot sauce (I like Crystal Hot Sauce)

½ tablespoon Worcestershire sauce

1 pound shrimp, peeled and deveined

Kosher salt

White pepper

1. In a large saucepan, heat the butter over medium heat. Add the Cajun Trinity, ½ cup of scallions, the garlic, and bay leaf and cook until soft and translucent.

2. Add the Cajun spice blend, thyme, parsley, paprika, and cayenne pepper, and stir well. Continue to cook for a few minutes.

3. Add the flour, stir to incorporate and absorb any liquid, and cook for 3 to 4 minutes, stirring, to make a quick roux. Whisk in the red wine, white wine, and seafood stock. Whisk until smooth. Bring to a boil, then reduce the heat to a simmer for 15 to 20 minutes. Add the hot sauce and Worcestershire sauce, and stir well. Fold in the shrimp and heat through until pink, then season with salt and white pepper to taste. To serve, garnish with the remaining ½ cup scallions.

HONEY AND CREOLE MUSTARD–GLAZED SALMON WITH PECANS

30 MINUTES

This salmon fillet is glazed with honey and Creole mustard, topped with chopped pecans, and broiled until done. I prefer wild-caught salmon because the farmed variety are given color enhancers to make their skin unnaturally pink, but you can use farmed salmon in this recipe.

MAKES 6 PORTIONS

PREP TIME: 10 minutes | COOK TIME: 10 minutes

2 tablespoons honey

2 tablespoons Creole mustard (I like Zatarain's)

6 (6-ounce) salmon fillets

1 tablespoon unsalted butter, melted

½ teaspoon Cajun Spice Blend (page 20)

¼ cup pecans, chopped

1. Preheat the broiler on a high setting. In a small bowl, combine the honey and Creole mustard until well mixed.

2. Place the fillets skin-side down on a baking sheet or broiler pan, and lightly coat with the melted butter.

3. Evenly brush the mustard mixture on the fillets, then season with the Cajun spice blend.

4. Sprinkle the pecans evenly among the fillets. Place the pan 6 to 8 inches from the broiler and cook for 8 to 10 minutes, or until the fish flakes easily with a fork. Serve immediately.

SUBSTITUTION TIP: You can change up this recipe by switching the fish. Any firm-fleshed fish will work, including red snapper, redfish, tuna, swordfish, or Spanish mackerel. For a completely different flavor, swap Steen's Cane Syrup for the honey.

SMOTHERED PORK CHOPS

Pork chops are a versatile protein—they can be substituted in just about any recipe that calls for chicken breasts. This mouthwatering pork chop is smothered with onions. Try serving it with sides of yellow rice and *petit pois*—which is French for very small green peas. **MAKES 6 PORTIONS**

PREP TIME: 10 minutes | **COOK TIME:** 55 minutes

6 bone-in pork chops,
   center cut

½ tablespoon Cajun Spice
   Blend (page 20)

2 tablespoons
   unsalted butter

2 cups onions, julienned

1 cup Beef Stock (page 16)

1 tablespoon
   Worcestershire sauce

1. Season the pork chops evenly on both sides with the Cajun spice blend.

2. In a large sauté pan or cast-iron skillet, melt the butter over medium-high heat. Add the pork chops in batches and cook on both sides until browned. Transfer to a plate.

3. Place the onions in the pan and cook over medium heat, stirring frequently, until softened and browned.

4. Transfer the pork chops back to the pan. Add the beef stock and Worcestershire sauce, stir well, cover, and reduce the heat to low. Simmer for about 30 minutes, or until the pork chops are tender. Serve immediately.

VARIATION TIP: You can swap out the pork for boneless chicken breasts. Cook the chicken until no pink remains and it reaches an internal temperature of 165°F.

SHRIMP-STUFFED BELL PEPPERS

Many stuffed pepper recipes call for parboiling the bell peppers, which makes them limp. Here, the peppers are cooked in a water bath to achieve the perfect firmness. For a vegetarian variation, use Vegetable Stock (page 17) and replace the shrimp with 1 cup of cooked chickpeas.

MAKES 8 PORTIONS

PREP TIME: 30 minutes | **COOK TIME:** 1 hour 15 minutes

4 large sweet bell peppers (red, yellow, or orange), halved

1 tablespoon unsalted butter

¾ cup Cajun Trinity, finely chopped (page 24)

1 tablespoon minced garlic

2 cups sliced mushrooms

1 tablespoon freshly squeezed lemon juice

1 cup diced tomatoes

1 cup cooked white rice

1 pound shrimp, peeled and deveined

½ cup Seafood Stock (page 18)

Kosher salt

White pepper

1 cup shredded Vermont cheddar cheese

½ cup shredded Parmesan cheese

½ cup warm water

1. Preheat the oven to 450°F. In a 9-inch square pan, place the bell pepper halves open-side up.

2. In a large sauté pan, melt the butter over medium heat. Add the Cajun Trinity and cook until soft and translucent. Add the garlic and cook, stirring frequently, for 1 minute. Add the mushrooms and lemon juice and cook until the mushrooms are soft. Add the tomatoes, stir well, cover, and cook for about 10 minutes.

3. Remove the cover and allow the moisture to reduce to almost dry. Add the rice, stirring well. Add the shrimp and cook until they are pink and heated through. Add the seafood stock and stir well. Season with salt and white pepper to taste.

4. Spoon the filling evenly among the peppers. In a small bowl, combine the Vermont cheddar cheese and the Parmesan cheese. Sprinkle the mixture evenly over the tops of the filled peppers.

5. Pour the water into the pan to make a ¼-inch layer of water around the peppers. Avoid getting any water in the peppers.

6. Cover the pan with heavy-duty aluminum foil and bake for 35 minutes. Remove the foil and bake for 10 more minutes, or until the cheese is melted and slightly browned. Serve immediately.

CHAPTER 5

SIDES AND SNACKS

These side dishes are the perfect accompaniment to any Cajun and Creole entrée. You'll find a quick recipe for Hushpuppies, which pair beautifully with any fried foods and are also a delicious snack between meals. Black Pepper Cheddar Biscuits are a twist on the classic Southern biscuits and gravy. One of my favorites, Baked Tomatoes, is great with Smothered Pork Chops (page 58) or Blackened Fish (page 44). Okra and Tomatoes is a traditional preparation using cut okra and diced tomatoes, both of which are abundant in Louisiana.

Collard Greens, page 69

HUSHPUPPIES

VEGETARIAN

According to the first historical accounts of hushpuppies in 1899, hunters and fishermen fed fried batter to their dogs to "hush the puppies." Always a great side for any seafood dish, hushpuppies are a regular lunch and dinner menu item served alongside fried catfish, fried shrimp, and fried oysters. Some restaurants offer hushpuppies with butter pats as a complementary treat instead of bread or rolls. **MAKES 24 HUSHPUPPIES**

PREP TIME: 10 minutes | **COOK TIME:** 5 minutes

2 teaspoons Cajun Spice
  Blend (page 20)

1 tablespoon
  chopped scallions

¼ cup granulated sugar

¼ cup finely
  chopped onion

½ cup all-purpose flour

⅓ cup whole kernel corn

¾ cup buttermilk

1½ cups self-rising
  yellow cornmeal

1 quart peanut oil

1. In a medium bowl, mix the Cajun spice blend, scallions, sugar, onions, flour, corn, buttermilk, and cornmeal and stir to combine well. Cover and refrigerate for 1 hour.

2. In a 3-quart stockpot or Dutch oven, heat the peanut oil to 350°F.

3. Using a tablespoon, form the mixture into small balls, drop into the hot oil, and fry for 2 to 3 minutes, turning several times to ensure even cooking, until golden brown.

4. Transfer to a plate lined with several layers of paper towels. Serve immediately.

PREP TIP: You can prepare the hushpuppy mix ahead of time, cover, and store in the refrigerator for several days until ready to fry.

BLACK PEPPER CHEDDAR BISCUITS WITH BLACK PEPPER GRAVY

30 MINUTES

These biscuits are quick to fix because they are rolled out and cut into squares, wasting no dough. Kneading and turning the dough produces flaky biscuits with thin layers. The cheddar cheese and black pepper are a great flavor combination. **MAKES 18 BISCUITS**

PREP TIME: 15 minutes | **COOK TIME:** 15 minutes

FOR THE BISCUITS

Nonstick cooking spray

2 cups all-purpose flour, plus more for dusting

1½ teaspoons baking powder

1 teaspoon freshly ground black pepper, divided

¼ teaspoon kosher salt

2 tablespoons unsalted butter, cold, cut into small pieces

¾ cup shredded sharp cheddar cheese

¾ cup buttermilk

1 large egg white, lightly beaten

TO MAKE THE BISCUITS

1. Preheat the oven to 425°F. Lightly grease a baking sheet with nonstick cooking spray and set aside. In a medium bowl, combine the flour, baking powder, ¼ teaspoon of black pepper, and the salt.

2. Cut in the cold butter with a pastry knife or pulse in a food processor until the mixture looks coarse and the butter is blended well into the dry ingredients. Add the cheese and mix well. Add the buttermilk and stir well to combine. Form a dough ball.

3. Put the dough ball onto a floured work surface and knead, turning five or six times. Roll the dough into a ½-inch-thick square, then use a chef knife to cut into 18 equal portions.

4. Place the biscuits on the prepared baking sheet, spaced about 1 inch apart. Brush each with egg white, then sprinkle evenly with the remaining ¾ teaspoon of black pepper.

5. Bake for 15 minutes, or until golden brown on top. Transfer to a platter and serve with black pepper gravy on the side.

INGREDIENTS CONTINUED >

CONTINUED >

BLACK PEPPER CHEDDAR BISCUITS WITH BLACK PEPPER GRAVY

CONTINUED

FOR THE GRAVY

3 tablespoons
  bacon grease

3 tablespoons
  all-purpose flour

2 cups milk, warmed

2 teaspoons freshly
  ground black pepper

1 teaspoon kosher salt

TO MAKE THE GRAVY

1. In a medium saucepan over medium heat, combine the bacon grease with the flour, stir well, and cook for 3 to 5 minutes to make a blond roux.

2. Add the milk, black pepper, and salt, using a whisk to incorporate the milk. Blend until smooth. Reduce the heat to low and simmer for 5 minutes, or until thickened. Serve immediately with the biscuits.

STORAGE TIP: You can make the gravy ahead of time, let cool, cover, and refrigerate for several days. Reheat in a saucepan over medium-low heat until it reaches a temperature of 150°F or starts to simmer on the edges.

PREPARATION TIP: Add the flour to the bacon grease in the same manner as when you make a roux. Start with a whisk to smooth out all the flour, then switch to a spoon and stir well to prevent scorching or burning.

INGREDIENT TIP: Gravy is typically made from the drippings of animal fats such as pork bacon and chicken or duck fat. You can substitute any animal fat or lard for the bacon grease. If you don't have any animal fat, use butter or peanut oil.

PUMPKIN SEED AND CHEDDAR CORNBREAD MUFFINS

ONE POT, VEGETARIAN

This twist on the ol' Southern favorite features roasted pumpkin seeds, cheddar cheese, and minced garlic. Top the halved muffins with butter or a drizzle of honey. **MAKES 12 MUFFINS**

PREP TIME: 10 minutes | **COOK TIME:** 25 minutes

Nonstick cooking spray

2 tablespoons granulated sugar

2 cups cornmeal

½ cup pumpkin seeds, roasted

1 large egg, beaten

1 cup milk

1 tablespoon melted butter

1 cup shredded cheddar cheese

1 tablespoon minced garlic

1. Preheat the oven to 400°F. Coat a 6-cup muffin pan with nonstick cooking spray and set aside. In a medium bowl, combine the sugar, cornmeal, and pumpkin seeds. In another bowl, combine the egg, milk, and melted butter and beat well together.

2. Mix the wet and dry ingredients and stir well until smooth.

3. Fold in the cheese and the garlic.

4. Portion the batter evenly among the muffin cups in the prepared pan.

5. Bake for 25 minutes, or until golden brown. Use a cake tester or toothpick to test for doneness. Serve immediately.

SIMPLIFY IT: You can make the batter ahead of time and refrigerate, covered, for several hours before baking. Take it out of the refrigerator and let it sit on the counter for about an hour before portioning out and baking.

BAKED TOMATOES

VEGETARIAN

These tomatoes are perfect with any main course. I recommend using beefsteak or full-size heirloom tomatoes. Tomatoes are full of lycopene, which can promote heart and eye health, and their fiber aids digestion.

MAKES 8 PORTIONS

PREP TIME: 10 minutes | **COOK TIME:** 30 minutes

1 cup mayonnaise

½ teaspoon garlic salt

½ tablespoon Creole
  Spice Blend (page 22)

½ tablespoon dried thyme

½ cup shredded
  Parmesan cheese

4 medium tomatoes

½ cup Italian
  bread crumbs

1. Preheat the oven to 425°F. In a medium bowl, combine the mayonnaise, garlic salt, Creole spice blend, thyme, and Parmesan cheese.

2. Cut the tomatoes into even halves and place in a 9-inch square baking dish. Spoon the mayonnaise mixture onto each tomato half and spread evenly.

3. Top each tomato with the bread crumbs. Bake for 30 minutes, or until the tomatoes are soft and their tops are golden brown. Serve immediately.

VARIATION TIP: You can add any of your favorite herbs or spices to the mayonnaise mixture. Try curry powder or a combination of chili powder and cumin. Replace the bread crumbs with seasoned crouton crumbs. Try using different heirloom tomatoes if you can find them in your market or if you grow your own.

SPICY GARLIC MASHED POTATOES

ONE POT, VEGETARIAN

Yukon Gold potatoes have a creamy texture and a rich flavor, especially paired with garlic. If Yukon Gold are not available, any young potato, such as new red, white, or yellow, will work for this recipe. **SERVES 8**

PREP TIME: 5 minutes | **COOK TIME:** 45 minutes

2 pounds Yukon Gold potatoes, skin removed, cut into 1-inch pieces, and rinsed

2 teaspoons kosher salt

8 tablespoons (1 stick) unsalted butter

¼ cup minced garlic

1 teaspoon garlic salt

½ teaspoon white pepper

½ tablespoon Cajun Spice Blend (page 20)

1 cup sour cream, tempered (see Ingredient Tip page 50)

½ cup cream cheese, softened

1. Place the potatoes in a 3-quart stockpot and add enough cool water to cover. Add the salt. Bring to a boil over medium-high heat and cook for 25 minutes, or until soft. When a small paring knife inserts easily into one of the larger pieces, they are done. Don't overcook the potatoes or they will start to break up too much. Drain well in a colander.

2. In the same pot, melt the butter over medium heat. Add the garlic and cook for 2 minutes. Add the garlic salt, white pepper, and Cajun spice blend, and cook, stirring frequently, for 3 minutes. (Do not brown the garlic.) Turn off the heat.

3. Add the potatoes and stir to coat.

4. Mash the potatoes, leaving some chunks. Fold in the sour cream and cream cheese. Serve immediately.

OKRA AND TOMATOES

DAIRY-FREE, GLUTEN-FREE, ONE POT, VEGETARIAN

Okra is also known as *quibombo* in Spanish and *gombo* in French. Slaves from West Africa introduced okra to the Caribbean and United States most likely in the 1700s, and the Creoles in Louisiana learned to thicken soups with it. Okra remains the essential ingredient in Creole gumbo, which is still widely enjoyed today. **SERVES 6**

PREP TIME: 15 minutes | COOK TIME: 50 minutes

1 tablespoon peanut oil

2 medium onions, diced large

6 garlic cloves, minced

3 cups fresh okra, cut into ½-inch slices

3 cups diced tomatoes

½ cup red wine vinegar

1 bay leaf

2 tablespoons Creole Spice Blend (page 22)

Kosher salt

1. In a 3-quart saucepan, heat the peanut oil over medium-high heat. Add the onions and cook for a few minutes, until soft and translucent.

2. Add the garlic, stir well, and cook for a few more minutes. Add the okra, tomatoes, and red wine vinegar and stir well to incorporate. Bring to a boil.

3. Add the bay leaf and Creole spice blend, stir well, reduce the heat to a slow simmer, and cover.

4. Cook for 30 minutes, stirring about every 10 minutes. Season with salt to taste. Serve immediately.

INGREDIENT TIP: Vinegar is added to many okra recipes because it helps break down the thick, slimy texture okra takes on after it has been cut and cooked.

COLLARD GREENS

ONE POT

This Southern favorite has a Cajun twist with andouille sausage, Cajun Trinity, and Cajun Spice Blend. Cane syrup and a touch of apple cider vinegar add sweet and sour notes. **SERVES 8**

PREP TIME: 20 minutes | **COOK TIME:** 1 hour 30 minutes

¼ **pound thick-cut bacon,** cut into 1-inch pieces

2 cups **Cajun Trinity** (page 24), diced

½ **pound andouille** sausage, diced

1 tablespoon **Cajun Spice** Blend (page 20)

2 tablespoons minced garlic

1 (½-pound) **smoked** ham hock

2 pounds **collard greens,** cut into 2-inch pieces

1 quart **Chicken Stock** (page 15)

¼ cup **cane syrup** (I like Steen's)

2 tablespoons **apple** cider vinegar

Kosher salt

Freshly ground black pepper

1. In a large 8-quart stockpot, brown the bacon over medium heat until crispy. Using a slotted spoon, transfer the bacon to a plate lined with several layers of paper towels. Keep the grease in the pot.

2. Add the Cajun Trinity and sausage and cook for 5 minutes, stirring frequently, until the Cajun Trinity is soft and translucent. Add the Cajun spice blend, garlic, and ham hock, stir well, and cook for 1 to 2 more minutes.

3. Add the collard greens and stir well. Add the chicken stock, cane syrup, and apple cider vinegar. Add the reserved bacon. Bring to a boil, then reduce the heat to a simmer and cook for 1 hour, until tender. Season with salt and black pepper to taste. Transfer to a large bowl and serve immediately.

BUTTERNUT SQUASH AND RAISINS

ONE POT, VEGETARIAN

Butternut squash has a sweet flavor. Tossed with melted butter and raisins, it goes well with pork, beef, and chicken. It's also great with roast turkey during the holidays. If you want to add some spices, see the Substitution Tip. **SERVES 8**

PREP TIME: 15 minutes | **COOK TIME:** 30 minutes

1 medium butternut
squash, peeled and cut
into 1-inch cubes

1 teaspoon kosher salt,
plus more for seasoning

2 tablespoons
unsalted butter

1 tablespoon light
brown sugar

1 cup raisins

White pepper

1. In a medium saucepan, cover the butternut squash with water, and add 1 teaspoon of salt. Bring to a boil, reduce the heat to a simmer, and cook until fork-tender. Drain in a colander.

2. In the same pan, melt the butter over medium heat. Stir in the brown sugar and raisins and cook for a few minutes.

3. Add the squash, stir well, and cook for a few minutes. Season with salt and white pepper to taste before serving.

SUBSTITUTION TIP: If you're a fan of cinnamon or you want to lend the dish some holiday flavor, add 1 teaspoon of ground cinnamon with the salt in step 1. A pinch of ground cloves and a sprinkling of nutmeg give the dish added excitement for Thanksgiving or Christmas. If you're looking for pizzazz, add 1 teaspoon of Creole Spice Blend (page 22) or a pinch or two of cayenne pepper.

CAJUN ROCKIN' ROASTED POTATOES

ONE POT, VEGETARIAN

This potato dish is perfect at a cookout or alongside grilled beef steaks, Smothered Pork Chops (page 58), Blackened Fish (page 44), and roasted or grilled chicken. Fresh rosemary and thyme are key to the success of this dish. Throwing in the cherry tomatoes at the end allows them to plump up but not break. **SERVES 8**

PREP TIME: 15 minutes | **COOK TIME:** 45 minutes

2 pounds new red
   potatoes, Yukon Gold
   potatoes, or any small
   creamer potatoes, cut
   into 1½-inch chunks

12 garlic cloves, sliced

2 cups pearl
   onions, peeled

¼ cup chopped
   fresh rosemary

¼ cup chopped
   fresh thyme

1 tablespoon Cajun Spice
   Blend (page 20)

2 tablespoons unsalted
   butter, melted

1 pint cherry tomatoes

1. Preheat the oven to 425°F. Put the potatoes in a 9-by-13-inch casserole dish. Add the garlic, onions, rosemary, thyme, Cajun spice blend, and melted butter. Toss well to coat evenly.

2. Bake for 45 minutes, stirring every 15 minutes. Use a small paring knife or the tines of a fork to test the doneness of several potatoes. Add the cherry tomatoes and gently toss. Bake for another 5 minutes, or until the tomatoes plump. Serve immediately.

SIMPLIFY IT: To prep ahead of time, toss all the ingredients except the tomatoes in a large bowl and refrigerate, covered, up to 2 days. When ready to cook, transfer to a casserole dish and pick up with step 2.

SESAME-SOY CAJUN GREEN BEANS

30 MINUTES, ONE POT

I developed this recipe one evening when my wife and I were reminiscing about the sesame green beans we used to order at one of our favorite Vietnamese restaurants. Sautéed in sesame oil with julienned red onions, these beans explode with flavor. **SERVES 8**

PREP TIME: 10 minutes | **COOK TIME:** 20 minutes

½ tablespoon sesame oil

1 cup julienned red onion

2 pounds fresh green beans, stemmed

2 tablespoons soy sauce

2 tablespoons oyster sauce

½ tablespoon Cajun Spice Blend (page 20)

½ teaspoon kosher salt

½ tablespoon toasted sesame seeds (see Ingredient Tip)

1. In a large sauté pan, heat the sesame oil over medium-high heat. Add the red onion and cook for 4 to 5 minutes, stirring occasionally, until soft and translucent.

2. Add the green beans and cook, stirring frequently, for 6 to 8 minutes, or until soft.

3. Add the soy sauce, oyster sauce, and Cajun spice blend, and stir well to coat. Cook, stirring occasionally, for a few minutes. Add the salt and toasted sesame seeds, and stir well until evenly mixed. Transfer to a platter and serve immediately.

INGREDIENT TIP: Served over rice, this dish is great with any meat entrée.

INGREDIENT TIP: To toast sesame seeds, put them in a medium sauté pan and toss gently over medium heat until they turn light brown. Toss or stir frequently so they brown evenly.

CHAPTER 6

SWEETS AND DESSERTS

Cajuns and Creoles love their sweets. This chapter includes two traditional French desserts: Crème Caramel made with an egg custard and caramel sauce, and Cream Puffs, both of which are still popular in and around Louisiana. Heavenly Hash Brownies is a family recipe handed down and enjoyed to this day, particularly around the holidays.

Cream Puffs, page 78

CRÈME CARAMEL

GLUTEN-FREE, VEGETARIAN

Originally from France, this classic has found its way into many homes in and around New Orleans, and although it's not specifically a Cajun or Creole preparation, there's no doubt it's a local treasure. For this recipe, you'll need 1-cup ramekins or soup cups to create individual servings. **SERVES 8**

PREP TIME: 20 minutes | COOK TIME: 1 hour

FOR THE CARAMEL SAUCE

1 cup granulated sugar

¼ cup water

FOR THE CUSTARD

¾ cup granulated sugar

12 large eggs

4 cups whole
    milk, warmed

2 teaspoons
    vanilla extract

½ teaspoon kosher salt

1 to 2 cups hot water

TO MAKE THE CARAMEL SAUCE

1. In a medium saucepan, combine the sugar and water. Whisk well, making sure no dry lumps of sugar remain. Bring to a simmer over medium heat, stirring, until the sugar is completely dissolved. Cover and reduce the heat to a simmer.

2. Continue simmering until the mixture reaches 310°F, otherwise known as the caramel stage. The sauce will have an amber color, then will progress to dark brown.

3. Remove from the heat and keep covered.

TO MAKE THE CUSTARD

1. Preheat the oven to 350°F. In a large bowl, combine the sugar and eggs and whisk until smooth. Slowly whisk in the milk. Continue stirring, until the sugar is completely dissolved. Gently stir in the vanilla and salt.

2. Divide the caramel sauce evenly among 8 serving ramekins or cups. Let cool and slightly solidify, then divide the custard mixture evenly, filling each ramekin about two-thirds full.

3. Set the ramekins in a roasting pan or on a baking sheet and add the hot water to the pan to create a bath around the ramekins. This prevents the custard from burning.

4. Bake for 25 minutes, or until a cake tester or tooth-pick inserted in the custard comes out clean.

5. Remove the ramekins from the water bath and let sit for at least 30 minutes.

6. When ready to unmold, run a small knife around the edges of one custard, then place it onto a small saucer or plate, turn it upside down, and shake gently to get it to release. The custard and caramel sauce will slide out and spread. Serve immediately.

SIMPLIFY IT: If preparing ahead of time, keep the custards in the ramekins. Once cooled to room temperature, cover and keep them refrigerated for up to 2 days, then follow the unmolding instructions in step 9.

CREAM PUFFS

VEGETARIAN

Popular in Louisiana around the winter holidays (and during Mardi Gras, with green, purple, and gold sugars sprinkled on top), these tiny morsels of cream-filled pastry are a charming addition to any dessert table. *Pâte à choux*, otherwise known as *choux paste*, is a classic French dessert preparation that goes back to 16th-century France. This light, versatile pastry dough is used for making sweet cream puffs, pastry swans, éclairs, croquembouches, and profiteroles. It's also a savory preparation for *gougères*, which are prepared with cheese. The high protein and gluten content of bread flour gives the choux paste body and allows the puffs to stand up. **MAKES 24 CREAM PUFFS**

PREP TIME: 25 minutes | **COOK TIME:** 35 minutes

FOR THE PÂTE À CHOUX

Parchment paper

1 cup water

8 tablespoons (1 stick) unsalted butter

½ teaspoon kosher salt

1 cup bread flour

6 large eggs

FOR THE WHIPPED CREAM

¼ cup granulated sugar

2 cups heavy (whipping) cream

½ teaspoon vanilla extract

TO MAKE THE PÂTE À CHOUX

1. Preheat the oven to 425°F. Line 2 baking sheets with parchment and set aside.

2. In a medium saucepan, bring the water, butter, and salt to a boil over medium-high heat. Remove from the heat and gradually stir in the flour, until fully incorporated and a solid ball is formed.

3. Return the pan to the heat and stir for 3 to 4 more minutes, until the dough pulls away from the sides of the pan.

4. Transfer the dough to a stand mixer bowl and let cool for 5 minutes. Fit the mixer with the paddle attachment. With the mixer on the lowest speed, add the eggs one at a time, making sure each one is fully incorporated before adding the next. Continue until all the eggs are added and the dough is smooth.

5. Transfer to a pastry bag and pipe out golf ball-size balls. If you don't have a pastry bag, spoon out the dough. Space the balls 2 inches apart on the prepared baking sheets.

6. Bake for 10 minutes, then reduce the heat to 375°F and bake for 10 more minutes, or until golden brown. Use a paring knife to pierce a small hole on the sides of each puff to release steam, then let cool to room temperature.

7. Transfer the whipped cream to another pastry bag. Fill each puff with the whipped cream by piping the cream into the small hole you created in step 5.

8. Transfer to a dessert platter and serve immediately, or cover with plastic wrap and refrigerate for up to 1 day.

TO MAKE THE WHIPPED CREAM

1. Place a stand mixer bowl and wire whisk attachment in the freezer for 10 minutes.

2. Put the sugar, cream, and vanilla in the bowl. Whisk at medium speed until stiff peaks form when you lift the whip attachment from the cream.

INGREDIENT TIP: If preparing ahead of time, store the whipped cream in an airtight container in the refrigerator for up to 6 hours. Gently whisk again by hand for several seconds before serving or piping.

CHOCOLATE MOUSSE

VEGETARIAN

Mousse is a French term meaning froth or foam, achieved by beating egg whites. This airy dish can be sweet or savory, hot or cold. This version is sweet and cold. It contains just three ingredients. **SERVES 6**

PREP TIME: 15 minutes

1 cup semisweet
  chocolate chips
1 cup heavy (whipping)
  cream, scalded
3 large eggs, separated

1. Place the chocolate chips in a food processor and blend until coarse like sand.

2. With the processor still running, slowly pour in the scalded heavy cream. Blend for 15 to 20 seconds, until the mixture is smooth.

3. One by one, add the egg yolks, running the processor for a few seconds to fully incorporate each one. Transfer to a large bowl and let the mixture cool completely to room temperature.

4. In a separate large mixing bowl, beat the egg whites until they are stiff and hold a slightly curved peak when you raise the whisk.

5. Using a rubber spatula, transfer about half the beaten egg whites to the chocolate mixture and stir gently. Repeat with the remaining egg whites, stirring gently, until incorporated.

6. Divide the mousse evenly among 6 serving dishes, then cover with plastic wrap and refrigerate for at least 4 hours. Serve within a day of preparation.

INGREDIENT TIP: For a hint of spice, add ½ teaspoon of ground cinnamon with the chocolate chips in step 1. If you want to make a mint-flavored chocolate mousse, add ¼ teaspoon of peppermint extract with the heavy cream in step 2.

FRESH BERRIES WITH CRÈME ANGLAISE

GLUTEN-FREE, 30 MINUTES, VEGETARIAN

This dessert features fresh strawberries, blueberries, and raspberries coated with sweet crème anglaise, the classic French dessert sauce.

SERVES 4

PREP TIME: 15 minutes | **COOK TIME:** 15 minutes

FOR THE CRÈME ANGLAISE

½ cup granulated sugar

4 large egg yolks, at
room temperature

1 teaspoon cornstarch

1¾ cups milk, scalded
(See Preparation Tip)

1 tablespoon
vanilla extract

TO MAKE THE CRÈME ANGLAISE

1. Fill a double boiler or saucepan with water and bring to a simmer.

2. In a small stainless-steel mixing bowl, place the egg yolks and gradually beat the sugar into them for 2 to 3 minutes, or until the mixture is pale yellow and forms a ribbon when you lift the whisk.

3. Add the cornstarch and beat so that it dissolves. While continuing to beat, very gradually pour in the scalded milk in a thin, steady stream, taking care that the yolks do not start to cook or congeal.

4. Put the bowl over the double boiler.

5. Using a rubber spatula or wooden spoon, stir continuously, reaching all over the bottom and sides of the bowl, until the sauce thickens just enough to coat the back of a spoon with a light, creamy, saucelike layer. Do not let the mixture come to a simmer; it should never get above 170°F.

6. Remove from the heat. Using a wire whisk, beat the sauce for 1 or 2 more minutes to cool. Strain through a fine sieve into another bowl. Beat in the vanilla.

7. Set the bowl of sauce in a larger bowl of cold water, stirring frequently, until cool. Cover and refrigerate.

INGREDIENTS
CONTINUED >

CONTINUED >

FOR THE BERRIES

2 tablespoons
   granulated sugar

1 tablespoon dark rum

1 cup strawberries, hulls
   trimmed and quartered

1 cup blueberries

1 cup raspberries

Fresh mint leaves,
   for garnish

TO MAKE THE BERRIES

1. In a small bowl, combine the sugar and rum and stir well, until the sugar is dissolved.

2. Add the strawberries, blueberries, and raspberries and toss until well coated.

3. Divide the berries among four serving dishes and lightly drizzle with the crème anglaise. Garnish with fresh mint and serve immediately.

PREPARATION TIP: Scalded milk has been heated to just below the boiling point to a low simmer, and until it shimmers on the sides of the pot.

STORAGE TIP: You can refrigerate the crème anglaise for several days, but this will make it thicker than you want. Before serving, set it out to come to room temperature. Stir it a bit to test the consistency, then add to your berries or other dessert creations.

LEMON SQUARES

VEGETARIAN

The southern regions of Louisiana have a temperate climate. Many farmers in Plaquemines Parish, just south of New Orleans, grow lemon trees. These lemon squares are perfect for potluck dinners. **MAKES 24 SQUARES**

PREP TIME: 15 minutes | **COOK TIME:** 50 minutes

8 tablespoons (1 stick)
   butter, melted
1 cup all-purpose flour
   plus 2 tablespoons
¾ cup confectioners'
   sugar, divided
2 large eggs, beaten
1 tablespoon lemon zest
2 tablespoons lemon juice
1 cup granulated sugar
½ teaspoon
   baking powder

1. Preheat the oven to 350°F. In a medium bowl, mix the melted butter, 1 cup of flour, and ¼ cup of confectioners' sugar with a spoon.

2. Evenly pat the crust into the bottom of a 9-inch square baking pan. Bake for 25 minutes, or until lightly browned. Keep the oven on.

3. In a medium bowl, whisk together the eggs, lemon zest, lemon juice, granulated sugar, remaining 2 tablespoons of flour, and the baking powder.

4. Pour the mixture over the crust.

5. Return to the oven and cook for 25 minutes, or until lightly browned on the sides and top.

6. Let cool completely. To serve, sprinkle the top with the remaining ½ cup of confectioners' sugar and cut into 24 even squares. For larger bars, cut into 12 squares.

PREPARATION TIP: Allow the eggs to come to room temperature before mixing. This gives them an airy, fluffy texture, which results in a smoother batter.

HEAVENLY HASH BROWNIES

The name of this recipe is derived from Elmer Chocolate's famous Heavenly Hash Egg, which is hard to find outside the Gulf Coast. My mother made this very recipe for every holiday gathering.

MAKES 18 SQUARES

PREP TIME: 10 minutes | **COOK TIME:** 30 minutes

1 (18-ounce) package brownie mix

1 cup chopped walnuts

2 cups mini marshmallows

8 tablespoons (1 stick) butter, melted

2 ounces baking chocolate

¼ cup milk

½ pound confectioners' sugar

1. Preheat the oven according to the package instructions. Prepare the brownie mix, and add the walnuts. Bake in an 8- or 9-inch square pan.

2. Remove from the oven and top with the marshmallows. Let melt slightly.

3. In a medium saucepan, combine the melted butter, chocolate, and milk over very low heat. Cook, stirring well, until the mixture melts together into a smooth consistency.

4. Transfer to a large bowl, then whisk in the confectioners' sugar to make chocolate icing. Pour the icing over the top of the marshmallows. Let sit for 2 hours before cutting to serve.

INGREDIENT TIP: These rich brownies go great with a hot cup of café au lait, or coffee with warm milk. If you don't like walnuts, substitute pecans or almonds.

New Orleans Seafood Chowder, page 48

MEASUREMENT CONVERSIONS

	US STANDARD	US STANDARD (OUNCES)	METRIC (APPROXIMATE)
VOLUME EQUIVALENTS (LIQUID)	2 tablespoons	1 fl. oz.	30 mL
	¼ cup	2 fl. oz.	60 mL
	½ cup	4 fl. oz.	120 mL
	1 cup	8 fl. oz.	240 mL
	1½ cups	12 fl. oz.	355 mL
	2 cups or 1 pint	16 fl. oz.	475 mL
	4 cups or 1 quart	32 fl. oz.	1 L
	1 gallon	128 fl. oz.	4 L
VOLUME EQUIVALENTS (DRY)	⅛ teaspoon	——	0.5 mL
	¼ teaspoon	——	1 mL
	½ teaspoon	——	2 mL
	¾ teaspoon	——	4 mL
	1 teaspoon	——	5 mL
	1 tablespoon	——	15 mL
	¼ cup	——	59 mL
	⅓ cup	——	79 mL
	½ cup	——	118 mL
	⅔ cup	——	156 mL
	¾ cup	——	177 mL
	1 cup	——	235 mL
	2 cups or 1 pint	——	475 mL
	3 cups	——	700 mL
	4 cups or 1 quart	——	1 L
	½ gallon	——	2 L
	1 gallon	——	4 L
WEIGHT EQUIVALENTS	½ ounce	——	15 g
	1 ounce	——	30 g
	2 ounces	——	60 g
	4 ounces	——	115 g
	8 ounces	——	225 g
	12 ounces	——	340 g
	16 ounces or 1 pound	——	455 g

	FAHRENHEIT (F)	CELSIUS (C) (APPROXIMATE)
OVEN TEMPERATURES	250°F	120°C
	300°F	150°C
	325°F	180°C
	375°F	190°C
	400°F	200°C
	425°F	220°C
	450°F	230°C

RESOURCES

CAJUN CHEF RYAN

Carriere, MS

CajunChefRyan.com

This blog is where I record, preserve, and share recipes collected from family, friends, and more than three decades' restaurant experience. My Cajun Spice Blend and Finger Lickin' Rub are available for sale here.

CAJUN GROCER

Metairie, LA

CajunGrocer.com

The Cajun Grocer offers just about any product you need to prepare Louisiana and New Orleans cuisine, including French bread, crawfish, boudin, Tasso ham, andouille, king cakes, sauces, spices, marinades, coffee, condiments, mixes, and frozen prepared meals.

CAMELLIA BRAND

Harahan, LA

CamelliaBrand.com

With a slogan of "Red Beans Done Right," Camellia has the best red beans, and it's the only brand I buy when I'm making a batch of red beans and rice. The product line includes lima beans, pinto beans, navy beans, great northern beans, black beans, field peas, green split peas, lentils, and many other products.

CENTRAL GROCERY & DELI

New Orleans, LA

CentralGrocery.com

Home of the famous Original Muffuletta Sandwich, Central Grocery also has a great selection of olive salads you can order for your own muffulettas.

ELMER CHOCOLATE

Ponchatoula, LA

ElmerChocolate.com

Famous for its Easter candies of Gold Brick Eggs, Heavenly Hash Eggs, Pecan Eggs, and Gold Brick Topping Sauce, Elmer Chocolate has been making and selling candy since 1855.

JACOB'S WORLD FAMOUS ANDOUILLE

LaPlace, LA

CajunSausage.com

In addition to its famous andouille sausage, Jacob's offers smoked sausage, Italian sausage, smoked chickens, smoked turkey wings, Tasso ham, boudin, hog crackling, and filé powder. Most products are sent via two-day mail; perishables are shipped overnight.

LOUISIANA SEAFOOD EXCHANGE

New Orleans, LA

LouisianaSeafoodExchange.net

From alligator meat to wahoo—and with crabs, crawfish, escargot, oysters, shrimp, or turtle meat in between—Louisiana Seafood Exchange has more than 90 fresh seafood selections and shipping is available to all 50 states.

STEEN'S SYRUP

Abbeville, LA

SteensSyrup.com

Steen's 100% Pure Cane Syrup is the main product, but they also offer Steen's Pure and Natural Dark Molasses and Southern Made Blended Syrup.

ZATARAIN'S

Gretna, LA

Zatarains.com

Crawfish, shrimp, and crab boil spices; Creole mustard; Creole seasoning; prepared horseradish; gumbo filé powder; fish fry; and root beer extract are just a few of the items from Zatarain's vast line of New Orleans flavors and products.

INDEX

W

ACKNOWLEDGMENTS

This cookbook would not exist without my dear wife, Monique Boudreaux, at my side every step of way. I cherish every moment we have together and enjoy extending the family culinary heritage together in our kitchen.

In memory of my mom, Martha Boudreaux, who will always be recollected for inspiring me in the home kitchen at an early age and giving me the courage to pursue a career in culinary arts.

My dad, Joseph Boudreaux, is recognized for his compassion for food, and though his own cooking is now limited, dining out together is a pure pleasure and always appreciated.

My sister, Wanda Boudreaux, who continues the family food traditions at her house.

My mother-in-law, Jeannette Boyer, for sharing the same passion for food, dining, and family recipes as well as the adored lunch or dinner out with family and friends.

Chef Lee Ambrose, who mentored me at the Hyatt Hotel during my apprenticeship and taught me all the soups, stocks, and sauces when I held the saucier position.

The late Chef Chris Canan, who took me under his wing at the Columns Hotel and taught me the fine art of smoked seafood and how to butcher chicken, duck, rabbit, and who introduced me to farm fresh herbs, edible flowers, and wild mushrooms.

Master Baker Instructor Chef Mark Fitch, for teaching me the science of pastries and baking while I was making my way through the culinary apprenticeship program at Delgado Community College.